I Believe
in Hope

I Believe in Hope

JOSÉ MARÍA DIEZ-ALEGRÍA

Translated by Gary MacEoin

Doubleday & Company, Inc.
Garden City, New York
1974

This book was originally published in Spain by Editorial Española Desclée De Brouwer (1972) under the title Yo Creo en la Esperanza
© Editorial Española Desclée De Brouwer

Excerpts from But That I Can't Believe by Anglican Bishop
    John A. T. Robinson,
A volume in Perspectives in Humanism, planned and edited
    by Ruth Nanda Anshen.
Copyright © 1967 by J. A. T. Robinson.
Reprinted by permission of Dr. Ruth Nanda Anshen.
Excerpts from The Jerusalem Bible, copyright © 1966 by Darton, Longman & Todd, Ltd., and Doubleday & Company, Inc. Used by permission of the publisher.
Excerpts from English translation of In Ioannis Evangelium are from Nicene and Post-Nicene Fathers, Grand Rapids, Michigan: William B. Eerdmans, 1956. Reprinted by permission.

ISBN: 0-385-08448-x
Library of Congress Catalog Card Number 73–82244
English Translation Copyright © 1974 by Doubleday & Company, Inc.
Printed in the United States of America
First Edition

Contents

CONTENTS

Explanatory Note

MY FRIENDS have asked me to explain how I live my Christian faith.

I have decided that I have no right to deny their request.

A Christian should be ready at all times to set out the grounds of his faith, and to do so publicly.

A crisis of faith exists among believers today. This imposes on those of us who believe the obligation to take the risk of setting out with complete sincerity the road our faith has taken, and how that faith stands today.

Only in this sincere dialogue of faith can we help ourselves and each other to continue forward.

I hope that the honest statement of my faith will help someone.

If anyone finds that my way of living my faith does not help him, he should put this book down. And if his charity is great, let him pray to God for me.

Faith is so mysterious and so "existential" (so "gratuitous") that we cannot all live it in the same way.

But what I regard as essential—today more than ever—is sincerity. Each one of us should ask himself sincerely what he believes and how he believes. And he should share his belief with others. He should have the courage to speak honestly.

EXPLANATORY NOTE

To remain silent because of fear or prudence, or to observe a teaching because that is what you were told to do, without a complete questioning of yourself about your own "faith," is to condemn that very faith to death.

The reason is that faith, to be truly faith, must be the most sincere and most personal element in the life of the believer.

Because this is so, I am writing this book on my own exclusive responsibility. I do this because what is at issue is not an academic work or a textbook.

The issue is a confession of faith, no more, no less.

If it teaches anyone anything, on the living level of faith, may God be praised.

I

The Unfolding
of My Faith

1. The Crisis

I EXPERIENCED A CRISIS OF FAITH when I was twenty-four or
twenty-five years old.

Just before my nineteenth birthday I had entered the novitiate
of the Society of Jesus. Two years later I took the religious vows.

I was studying philosophy when the crisis of faith hit me. The
crisis was provoked specifically by my philosophical reflection.

Problems related to Kantian criticism, with the choice between
idealism and realism, together with skepticism and relativism, un-
derlay the crisis.

Looked at from today, the concerns of that period may seem to
me rather ingenuous. But there was a real problem, one that any
thinking person must face at all times, at the root of the crisis. Is
man capable of absolute knowledge and absolute certainty?

If man is not able to say "yes" without any reservation, and at
the same time with honesty, the possibility of an act of faith that
can be posited as an absolute "yes" does not exist.

For that reason, the intrinsic nature of my crisis of faith was
profound. When I look back, a full thirty-five years later, I do not
deny it.

9

The crisis lasted for about a year. It was for me a year of bitter suffering.

I believe that my vocation to the religious life had been substantially genuine, and as free and personal as was possible in the circumstances of those times.

During my five years of religious life, I had constructed for myself a certain level of interior life, perhaps somewhat conventional and forced, still with a dimension of sincerity that related it to what was vital and human within me, to what I might call my deepest biographical self. This interior life was for me Jesus, the Christ, believed by me to be alive and to be near at hand. With aspects of immaturity, of insincerity, of conventionalism and of "something forced," no doubt; but also with a nucleus of sincerity and of "lived" life, I applied to myself the words of Paul: "For me to live is Christ."

This may convey some idea of the trauma I experienced when my crisis of faith started. A young man of twenty-five, reasonably normal, reasonably alive and not at all turned in on himself had built his life around a living Christ present within him, only to find this Christ suddenly dissolve in smoke.

It was a year of intense suffering.

I loved my Christ, and I did not want to lose my faith.

But neither could I surrender my honesty. I could not close my eyes in order to continue to affirm my faith, unless I truly knew whether or not I believed. I had to keep my eyes open to the darkness of my faith. What I did was to wait, not to close out the matter with a "I have lost the faith."

In this way, after months of torment, the paradoxical solution turned up, what I here call "the unfolding of my faith."

One day the crisis of faith ended. I am not sure if this happened in a flash, or rather through some process without clearly defined outlines, but in any case, quite quickly. Jesus began to shine forth once more deep inside me, the living Christ. I was again able to say "yes" with honesty and sincerity, and with a grasp on the absolute. A certain kind of peace, which I had lost months earlier, returned.

But here comes the paradox. The doubts raised by philosophic reflection continued to be present, at their own level. I had not resolved them.

This caused the inmost reality of my faith to appear as something radically different from what I had been given to understand by courses of apologetics that were more interested in conclusions than in truth.

In concrete terms, the entire thrust of our training had been to establish that philosophy and the sciences of history proved with absolute certainty nothing less than the truth of the Catholic faith(!). Once this had been proven to him by reason and the sciences of history, a man could and should accept the faith. The "yes" of faith was affirmed on a different and higher plane (because it was an act of homage to "God revealing himself"), but it presupposed (as a "starting point") the absolute "yes" of the reason responding to a logically certain argument.

The way I now saw it, the absolute "yes" of faith rested on its own foundation, and there was no absolute "yes" of reason. The only absolute "yes" was that of faith.

I believe "because God has so revealed," but this "because" is also faith and nothing else. Revelation is within the person and existential. That is the only way in which faith is possible.

For the believer this faith is "charis." It is a grace. And that is all he needs.

I believe that every human knowledge of a rational nature, if it is honest and truly intelligent, finds itself expressed in the "yes" of the judgment with a margin of agnosticism. At times there is only a margin. The basic attitude of human understanding is to question rather than to affirm. It presents a question with an answer (with an affirmation), but the framework is the question. And the answer is not definitive, because the question always remains as a context that cannot be stripped away from the answer.

Faith is something quite different. It is an absolute "yes" in which a man goes outside himself to find himself in the person "in whom he believes."

From the time of the crisis of faith that I have been describing, I began consciously "to believe in Jesus Christ." I believed before, but I did not know that I believed. My self-awareness of my faith had not been brought to my attention.

This "unfolding of my faith" was rich in consequences that have continued to unfold themselves during my entire subsequent life. At the time it happened, I was not able to appreciate the extent and depth of those consequences. But I now can see that they were already in existence at that time.

Faith, as I have since lived it, is above all else "freedom." It means freedom in relation to everything that is human, and that includes the ecclesiastical or "institutionalized religion." It is a freedom of the spirit that makes it possible to face—at the appropriate level—the problems raised by history, by philosophy, or by science, and that with a total absence of prejudices. The reasons is that faith is now above all such matters. It no longer "rests on them."

Paul says that faith is "obedience," and that Christ makes us his "slaves" in faith. My own experience confirms for me that this is absolutely so. But that "obedience" makes us totally and absolutely free with regard to everything that is not Christ.

Faith does not bring us—at least, not necessarily—to deny the ecclesiastical institution, concretely that of the Catholic Church, or to cease to recognize an institutional kind of obedience, but it reduces such elements to the instrumental level.

Obedience to an ecclesiastical institution is not a supreme value such as to make of it some kind of foundation for one's faith in itself. It is a value subordinated to "the obedience which is faith." And that obedience which is faith binds me to Christ and gives me a dimension of liberty with respect to all else. Within that dimension of liberty there is room for obedience to an ecclesiastical institution, but perhaps not in the way in which the "apparatus" of the Catholic Church often understands and seeks it.

I'll come back later to these issues.

At this point all I want is to insist on the liberating power that the "unfolding of my faith" represented for me. This liberating power enabled me to face and to accept without trauma the enormous and extremely rapid change experienced by Catholic theology and the Catholic ecclesial reality in the past ten years (especially in those years).

2. Interior Solitude

THE END OF MY CRISIS of faith brought a deep peace and a conscious power to my life and personality.

This situation was, nevertheless, accompanied for a time by a sense of being alone and unable to communicate with others.

I was living in a community with other students. All of them were good confreres and brothers in our religious fellowship. That, at least, is how I found them. I have always found it easy to get along with others, and I think I don't make undue demands on people. I am not suspicious by nature.

But I was unable to find, even within the circle of my closest friends, a single one whose understanding could fill the sense of emptiness with which my wound tormented me.

Neither did faith, nor Christ, nor God the Father fill the deep void in my soul. Christ was firmly in my soul through my faith. But he was there as "an absense."

And this interior solitude, this inability to get outside myself in an interpersonal communication that would fulfill me, was like being choked painfully to death.

I began to write some poems—nothing very important—in which I tried to express what I was experiencing. I remember writing one called An Interior Psalm, which described the depths of my experience during those years.

I saw myself being drawn relentlessly, like a boat, toward the distant darkness of a fathomless sea. I had to drag myself away, sorrowing, from my friends: "Farewell, farewell my dear friends, you who are staying behind on the shore, strange and alien figures gesticulating in a distant light." This verse, the opening stanza of the psalm, still lingers in my memory. From the solitude of my boat, through the darkness, I stretched out my hand. But I could nowhere find the hand of another, and neither could I find in myself the money I would have liked to give my brother. Thus I saw myself forced to remain seated in the prow, absorbed in thought and silent, "my cheek resting on my hand, and my eyes lifted up to the stars." My silence was an ardent prayer, but it was completely shrouded in darkness. Like a beclouded light, my faith was still burning. And I waited hopefully.

During those same years I felt a very strong call to the foreign missions. This enthusiasm grew to the point of filling my life in an extraordinary way.

A kindly superior, who unfortunately was also inept and vacillating, left me under the impression that my youthful desire would quickly be realized. Then, with no warning or explanation, the plan was canceled. The disappointment for me was overwhelming, perhaps out of all proportion, but nonetheless real. My spontaneous reaction was to think of myself as a lover whose fiancée had for no reason been suddenly slain.

My sense of being alone was reinforced and became more bitter than ever. My favorite reading during those years was *Qoheleth* (Ecclesiastes).

I had completed my philosophy studies with a master's degree, and I had been sent to a residential high school as a teacher and student supervisor. I was not temperamentally suited to the supervisory work, and for a year I was constantly in a state of anxiety. I was depressed, and this undoubtedly affected my physical health, because at the end of the year I had to have minor surgery for a suppurating gland in my neck.

I thought a lot about death in those years. It was the theme of a short poem I wrote for a friend, a man older than I who was being sent to South America and for whom leaving home was difficult.

> Just to give you one thought in a few words
> As you are about to set sail:
> Forward like a man! Later on
> How beautiful it will be to die!

And for myself I wrote some lines in the depression of a sweltering summer.

> Lord, this dreadful fatigue I endure,
> What can it be?
> Is it possible that I find myself
> Already close to the jaws of death?

Combined with the thought of death I had a sense of emptiness. The disillusionment was profound.

There was a kind of terrace at the back of the school, with a view of open fields beyond. It is a somber but peaceful landscape. A country road winds gently up the slope. Trees shade the silent cemetery to the left. A low mountain range forms the background. In the evening the golden light adorned this landscape with beauty, but a beauty veiled for me in deep melancholy. I was a great admirer of the Spanish poet, Antonio Machado, and I tried to express how I felt in verses that were a pale imitation of his genius.

> One golden evening in May
> on the road to the cemetery.
> My love and my thoughts
> are nothing.
> Silver winds carried them away
> on the road to the cemetery.
> Myself they left dead
> beside the silent pathway;
> and away they went
> with not even a goodbye.

An excessively severe superior, a man who was not always consistent and at times almost inhuman, dealt with me harshly and with a lack of understanding that would be difficult to imagine. His harsh methods caused me to react in ways that proved beneficial for me. I learned to control my temper. I was forced to reaffirm my faith. I saw the need to remain open to love of my neighbor in spite of the natural pressure to withdraw.

I believe I reached a more realistic attitude and a more tranquil acceptance of the closed perspective within which I was then living.

At the end of this period of night, the fire of my faith was still burning or glowing obscurely. A short poem written on the eve of his ordination to the priesthood of one who then was and still is a close friend touches on this theme:

> Two hovering angels.
> Two candles, upright
> spears of peace,
> lowly lanterns.
> Bread and wine.
> A miracle
> profoundly simple.
> Here on earth
> the word is vigilant
> for the faith.

That is how things stood when I ended my work as a high school teacher and started to study theology. I was twenty-nine years old.

3. Precursors of the Dawn

THE PEACEFUL ATMOSPHERE of the theological studies, which moreover I found fascinating, brought a deep calm after the years of personal anguish I had experienced while teaching in the high school.

I read all the works of St. John of the Cross, and they affected me deeply.

I began—at a modest level—to find ways to engage in contemplative prayer and create an area of inner silence in which I felt God's presence. The result was a revolution in my life.

I believe my attempts at contemplation had an artificial and nervous element in them. And there was a degree of immaturity in my very modest experience of God's presence.

Here, nevertheless, I see an essential part of my life as a Christian. The feeling of being with God has stayed with me for thirty years. The night was behind me.

I would simply add that for years it is more than a "feeling." It is, I believe, something deeper and also more difficult to express in words. I can only call it a dimension of my existence.

I have had no positive desire, for many years now, to become a contemplative.

My faith is explicit, and my prayer to God—in the Eucharist and in other ways—is something I need in order to live. But I have replaced systematic efforts to carry on prayer of contemplation with the reading of the Bible, which as a whole and in one way or another is for me the word of God.

In addition, the modern trend among Christians to stress the "horizontal" dimension of life more than the "vertical" has also influenced me.

The trend of Christianity, as it is lived today, is not to flee the world in order to dig down into the mine within us, but rather to open up to the world and to men as the way to establish contact with the God hidden within them.

The axis of Christian life in our times is not solitary contemplation, as it was practiced by the anchorites in the desert. Rather the axis of Christian life for us is brotherly love (agape), a love of our neighbor open to all men.

If we are called to the desert, it is not as isolated individuals, but as members of an entire people moving forward together, as in the Exodus.

I quite agree that we have among the devout and among those who practice their religion with total faithfulness many who retain the vertical approach. But the dynamism of history, the "growth standard," points in the direction of an increase in the horizontal dimension, a movement away from the verticalism in vogue. This is true even among those Christians who retain an explicit faith in transcendence and in the value of prayer as an existential dimension of Christianity. I am one of those Christians. But the ways in which I pray have become more temperate. And I have lost—or left behind—an earlier concern for continual self-awareness, or what used to be called "recollection."

The impact of these changes has been to make my modest experience of the presence of God less easy to define but possibly more "existential."

It is as if the uttermost depths of my consciousness signified "not to be alone" and to be "caught up." But this awareness expresses itself so spontaneously and peacefully that I suspect the roots of the existential situation have bored down into the subconsciousness. I am, however, no expert in such matters.

The comparison that comes to me, when I try to explain to myself this way of "being with God," is that of the enveloping presence of the maternal womb. It is an atmosphere and a root sustaining me, which enter so intimately into the totality of my being that I am not even aware of their presence. But I, having lived through the night, know well how different it is to move in the light of these "precursors of the dawn."

I see clearly that this foundation of an existential "living with God" has the quality of a fertile soil, which gives to formal prayer and to the explicit and active awareness of my faith a deeper content and a new form of expression. Its principal characteristic is that it is no longer my prayer that sustains the presence of God, but the presence of God that gives meaning to my prayer. The reason is that the presence of God is not a "feeling" but an "existential datum," by which I mean a transcendental "situation" of my concrete existence.

I have, at the same time, a very clear understanding that this is all a grace (charis). It is not in my power to keep it. But I live in the hope of not losing it. That is because in the utmost depths of that "presence of God," there is an unshakable and consequently peaceful hope.

Let me end with a concrete recollection. In July 1969, at the end of a series of talks to priests in Yugoslavia, I stayed on for a day to take a look at Dubrovnik. The highlight was the tour of the wall, right over the sea, recalling the medieval battlements. I was all by myself as I enjoyed the spectacle, but surrounded by young couples, who were swarming all over the place. I felt a bond of understanding with those boys and girls, who were not at that moment involved in love-making, just simply enjoying the sun, the sea, and the beauty of the castle, yet always within a framework of friendly companionship with erotic overtones. For my part, I was viewing the scene without any trace of bitterness or sense of nostalgia as a lone individual among so many couples living an hour of happiness. Yet I felt no need to actualize the presence of God, in the ascetic sense, in order not to be alone. In the same way as those young people in that place and at that time were not making love, but simply enjoying the afternoon and the view—and that in the full personal experience of being in the other's company to the extent to which each attained it—so I similarly strolled along "having a companion," living this togetherness without having to think about it in terms of an artificial discipline.

Such is the existential perspective in which my faith is unfolding as a way of life.

4. The Christ of My Faith

I BELIEVE in Jesus of Nazareth, in the man Jesus who lived in history, who forms part of the human race.

My faith is a personal relationship with the man Jesus, a real and concrete man like me.

But, for that very reason, I do not reach Jesus through historical knowledge of Jesus, through the science of history. If I did, I would be unable to relate to him with the personal relationship that my faith constitutes.

I am profoundly interested in and indeed captivated by the historical study of Jesus, the analysis of the sources. I am enriched by the results of such study, results that can also be incorporated into my lived reflection on my faith. But my faith does not depend on the results of historical studies, if for no reason other than that such results never reach the level of lived certainty with which my faith knows and affirms Jesus. The certainty of the existence of Jesus that I acquire from history is completely different from the certainty of the shared reality that Jesus has for me in the interpersonal relationship of faith.

Historical knowledge is, consequently, not a support of faith —not even as regards the most central nucleus of the historic existence of Jesus, a nucleus historically established so absolutely that it would be preposterous to doubt.

Historically, that is to say, from the viewpoint of human historical knowledge and the science of history, the extent of the strictly historic nucleus within the synoptic gospels will always remain an open question. The extent may be very considerable, perhaps not. The question is open.

But the effort to insist that the claim that this nucleus is very extensive cannot be questioned, on the ground that faith could not be sustained unless this proposition is affirmed as an historical certainty, seems to be based on a misunderstanding of what faith is. It may also mean a misunderstanding of the meaning of historical study.

I believe in Jesus of Nazareth. And my faith in this living Jesus is a revelation that the Father was pleased to grant me. I believe that every genuine faith, whether or not the believer is conscious of the fact, is analogous to the mysterious faith of Paul.

Faith in Jesus is an interpersonal relationship that always has deeper roots than any intellectual proposition regarding Jesus.

Faith in Jesus, however, includes an appreciation of Jesus, a strictly unique and incomparable appreciation of him. Jesus is concretely a man, and at the same time he is above measure—an obvious mystery, but one into which I enter by faith more than I could enter into any neighbor physically living beside me, a mother, a father, a sweetheart, a friend.

The affirmations I make to myself (and that I can make to others) in order to "explain" my faith are always based on this radical "appreciation" of Jesus, which is the precise relationship of faith "in" Jesus, and which is always more than its conceptual expression. The conceptual expression takes place, like a man stuttering, within the interpersonal (appreciative) relationship that is faith "in" Jesus.

That is how I understand the following profession of my faith in Jesus:

I believe that Jesus is the anointed of the Father (the Christ), the one who was sent (the Messiah).

I believe that Jesus is the redeemer of men, the one in whom the world is saved.

I believe that Jesus died and rose from the dead. His death (undertaken in the fullness of love for the Father and for men) and his resurrection are a victory over our sin and our death. The "how," the "when" (or the process of "whens"), and the "why" of this victory are mysterious beyond all measure. Also mysterious is the reality that the death and resurrection of Christ constitute a "reconciliation" of men with men and with the Father.

I believe that Jesus is the Son of God. And I believe this to be a reality of such a nature as to constitute an unfathomable mystery. It is not possible to analyze it conceptually. The most that can be done is to glimpse incomprehensible depths of pre-existence, of glorification, of final expectation of fullness, but without being able to reach (scarcely) to the stuttering of propositions that can have any real "meaning."

I believe that Jesus, by his resurrection, has received the power to send out upon men the life-giving Spirit, together with the Father.

I believe that Jesus was sent by God "born of woman" in a truly human condition, and that this is an element in the mystery of salvation.

I believe that Jesus gives believers his body and blood in the bread and wine of the Eucharist. This is so true that it is for that very reason beyond understanding. It is believable, and it can be lived. But every attempt at analytical conceptualization—and perhaps even more so within a polemical frame of reference—removes from us the possibility of grasping the truth existentially, and that is the only way to reach it.

I believe that Jesus Christ is Lord and the "Lord of History," and that this is a constitutive dimension of the mystery of his resurrection.

This last statement will be the object of later reflection.

Regarding the other statements, I should add a further comment.

Many modern Christians have trouble in admitting the reality of the resurrection. In consequence, the tendency is growing to demythologize the content of faith in the resurrection, in the sense of overcoming the scandal of a realistic affirmation of the resurrection, thereby reducing it—as faith content—to the category of existential "value," something real in the consciousness of the believer.

I am not going to get into polemics, much less to condemn. One reason among others is that we quickly become trapped in almost insuperable language problems. That is why I have not risked going farther than to speak of a "tendency." In any case, the function that this tendency (whether real or supposed) performs for me here is to help me to clarify the way in which I live my faith in regard to this point.

I affirm the resurrection with a realism that makes the affirmation "scandalous" and "crazy." I do not reject the scandal and folly of my faith. But I do insist on its mysterious character. The content of what I affirm in my faith is literally unimaginable. The human understanding is unable to contain it. My absolutely firm affirmation is like a pointing finger, or like an arrow that disappears from sight into the night and that we recognize to have hit a target that we are unable to distinguish in the darkness.

I will go still farther. Faith in the resurrection is a faith-hope. (On the level on which I am reflecting about my "faith in Christ," faith-hope-charity are inseparable.) In this faith-hope in the resurrection, the existential pole of grasping the mystery on the part of the believer is hope more than faith.

It is our own resurrection that is the object of hope. And Jesus is the certain guarantee of that hope. Because of Jesus, the hope of our resurrection is asserted (lived) as a firm hope and not as "illusory." This reality of our hope includes the fact—the unthinkable fact—of resurrection; the resurrection of Jesus the first fruit, and our resurrection as the fullness that is to come.

In the existential order, we have to reach the more intellectual affirmation of the resurrection by the way of hope (which is more vital).

The resurrection is not a problem of knowledge, but of life. The response to the problem of life is hope. And Jesus Christ is our hope. But, because of that, our hope is not illusory. It is real. And through it we know (in faith) the reality of the resurrection.

In "faith in Jesus" we live the faith-hope of the resurrection (of Jesus and of ourselves). The Easter apparitions gave the disciples hope. Such hope contains and increases the tranquillity of faith for the simple reason that it is a "consistent" hope.

In the beautiful formulation of the Letter to the Hebrews, hope is the anchor that reaches right through beyond the veil to the mystery where Jesus entered before us. And our soul is bound to this anchor of hope (Heb. 6:19–20).

II

The Discovery
of True Religion

1. Crisis of Conscience

IN 1947 I BEGAN TO TEACH ETHICS in the philosophy faculty of the
Society of Jesus in Madrid. In my course I had to deal with the
basic problems of social ethics, work, the ownership of material
goods, and the principles of political ethics, both national and
international.

The ideological conditioning I had received as a Spaniard belonging to the Catholic middle classes, as a priest, and as a member of the Society of Jesus was clearly (and uncompromisingly)
conservative.

I had, nevertheless, a certain honesty that made me interpret
the so-called social doctrine of the Church (encyclicals of Leo
XIII and Pius XI and the discourses of Pius XII) in relatively
open terms.

Still there was a kind of lack of realism about the way I en-
visioned these social realities. I failed to see that, in spite of the
fact that the theses I defended were still overconservative, these
same theses—once understood in a dimension of realistic con-
creteness and a vital realization of their content—would inevitably
lead me to a critical attitude, and ultimately to some kind of

24

militant attitude, with regard both to capitalist society and to the historic significance that the Catholic Church has had, particularly in the past 150 years, and that it continues to have.

The step from an abstract view to a concrete comprehension was taken by me in Germany during the fall of 1955. After eight years of intense teaching activity, I had six months of complete freedom to reflect by myself outside Spain. The result was a kind of self-clarification, which forced me to recognize as harsh and urgent realities the problems I had previously been examining in the abstract, as in a dream.

That was the start of an awareness that has grown clearer and more personal in the following years. I felt myself involved, by my actions and by my omissions, in a series of collective responsibilities. What was even more shocking, I was involved precisely as a Catholic, a priest, and a Jesuit. There developed in me an urgent need to be really on the side of justice and against injustice, against oppression and in favor of true freedom for everyone, but above all for those who are most unjustly oppressed. There developed in me the obligation in conscience to "adopt a dissenting stand" within the Church and the society to which I belonged.

Such was the start of an undertaking in which I believe I have accomplished something, while knowing that I have not done nearly enough.

The starting point of my exodus (my wandering in the desert in search of the promised land) can be fixed as a public lecture I gave in the Madrid Chamber of Commerce on April 5, 1956, to an audience of middle-class Catholics. The lecture started with an exposition of the issues in these words:

1. In Spain we enjoy an apparent social peace, which is based not on a solid equilibrium but rather on political power; and underneath that surface peace lie the deep discontent and muffled hostility of the workers, a hostility that is largely justified. 2. Worker ill will is directed also against the Church, though perhaps in a lesser degree. 3. Wage levels established by law are largely unjust

in principle, because they are excessively low, and the recently decreed increase has not changed that situation substantially. 4. In the most general terms, the employers do not even ask themselves if they should pay more than the legal minimum; they think that is enough, and there have even been cases of fraudulent violation of the law. 5. The makeup and methods of action of ecclesiastical institutions have been no different in this area (let us assume that they have not been breaking the law). At least the Church has not been giving the impression that it operates any differently from the employer class. 6. The Spanish worker, who is often ill-mannered and uninstructed in how to behave (though it is proper to ask who is responsible for this state of affairs), is very often treated as an inferior being with whom it is not necessary to observe the ordinary rules of consideration for the feelings of others. That represents a breach of basic ethical and moral rules, a breach for which one cannot plead reasons of impossibility, as might be done in the case of wages. 7. The Spanish worker has in fact no effective way of promoting his rights to secure for himself a proper work situation, being forced to adjust passively to whatever the more or less efficacious good will of the government provides. 8. In the past twenty years, Spanish Catholicism taken as a whole and viewed in its various organizational forms has remained practically silent about these problems, probably because the issue was a thorny one and unpleasant for most people other than the workers, for whom it is a very serious question indeed.

Today this may seem a very weak formulation of the issues. But to speak like that in 1956 was a daring innovation both for me and for my audience. The text of the talk was sent to all the bishops and to other public figures.

That same year a national congress on the state of perfection and the apostolate was held in Madrid for priests and nuns. The organizing committee asked me to make a presentation on the subject, "The social aspect of the vow of poverty." I submitted my text to the committee, and the text was mentioned at the meeting. But when the proceedings appeared, it was not included. Here is what I wrote:

The evangelical basis of the vow of poverty has traditionally and correctly been referred to the words of Christ, when he said:

"If you wish to be perfect, go and sell what you own and give the money to the poor, and you will have treasure in heaven; then come, follow me." (Mt. 19:21).

Today perhaps the biggest problem facing the Catholic Church is its absence from the masses of the people, particularly from the workers. This is a problem about which the top level of the Church's hierarchy has voiced concern. People of the lower class, to a considerable extent, come to the Church as to something alien, something belonging to the middle classes, which they see— and with much reason—as a strange and other world.

What is needed is to win once more for Christ this world of the common people, the world specifically of those who are weary and heavy burdened, to whom the invitation of the Heart of Jesus is directed.

In the present order of providence, the theology of the redemption is organically related to the theology of the incarnation. To redeem us, Christ was incarnated in mankind. Without incarnation there is no redemption, and this is equally true of the Church's life in the apostolate.

Now, it is a fact that the Church, particularly in this country, has in recent years increased impressively its apostolic works for the poorer segments of society, activities intended to promote the work of redemption. Yet it is equally true that it has achieved only minimal *incarnation* into these same humble classes.

A suburban parish, a professional school, or a social welfare agency in a working-class district is often, if I am not mistaken, the work *of* a world distinct from the world of working men, established *for* the benefit of that world of working men. The people who live in those districts see the Church's activities as something coming from a different social domain, with the object of aiding them. The people who operate these institutions (the priests, doctors, teachers, etc.) are not in an unequivocal sense their neighbors, companions, or spouses. They do not share in the same fate. They are people from another world, of a different class, living within different social structures. They are here simply to help, even if they happen to have pitched their tent permanently among those they are protecting. I am not saying that all our institutions fit this description. But I do believe that here and now that is our standard mode of action.

Communism, by contrast, functions integrally by means of a system of cells, which accomplishes fully the method of incarnation. Communism establishes itself radically and universally as a movement *of* the workers, *of* the common people, as well as *for* them. Communism, as is obvious, has no backing among the middle classes. Over against them, it springs from the world of the workers and lives in it. More precisely, it is originally created by intellectuals, propagandists, and others who have been incarnated into the world of the workers and live as part of it.

As long as the duel between Catholicism and communism is set up with these sociological presuppositions, Catholicism can never win a substantive victory. Specifically, the experience of the Spanish Church during the past twenty years confirms the truth of this assertion. Approaches, such as the Young Christian Workers, which have made significant progress in the direction of bringing Christ's redemption to the world of the workers, have been possible because they were able to solve fully the problem of incarnation. Taking into account the fact that the masses of the people in Spain are much more de-Christianized than those of other countries, we have not succeeded in making any worthwhile impact because we are very far behind in our attempts to solve this problem of incarnation. Looked at in this perspective, the Spanish Church would have great difficulty in escaping the description of being overwhelmingly middle class.

A great part of the rank and file of the Spanish clergy come from working-class homes. Nevertheless, the processes by which these elements are incorporated and absorbed into the clergy detaches them from their world of origin and incardinates them into an ecclesiastical world which, sociologically speaking, is alien to the world of the proletariat and represents the front lines of the contact of the middle-class world with the proletariat.

Seen in the perspective of the apostolate, this is a dangerous situation and constitutes a serious problem.

Having come so far, a question is in order. The religious orders are the bodies that as institutions and as a state in life profess poverty in the Church. Would it not seem to be their special task to realize in an institutional and stable way the process of incarnation of the Church into the world of the poor? That is the question. But in fact nothing of the sort is taking place. I am well aware that some religious institutions, by contrast with the one to which I belong, have undoubtedly a more popular character and are more fully inserted into the people existentially and sociologically. Nevertheless, I do not feel that in Spain we have enough real examples of this kind of incarnation. In addition, the number of religious institutions of both men and women—especially those devoted to education—that are incarnated exclusively in the middle-class world and that try to perform a redemptive work among the workers without first being incarnated into their world, is sufficiently big to be called a problem. From this follows the unfortunate tendency, widespread among us, of relegating work with the poor to an accessory and subordinate category in the organization of our apostolic labors.

Let us go back to the original point of establishment of the state of perfection in the gospel. "If you wish to be perfect, go and sell what you own and give the money to the poor, and you will have treasure in heaven; then come, follow me." The whole machinery of poverty here brought into play is directed totally and efficaciously toward the incarnation of the apostle into the world of the poor. His first step is to distribute his goods among the poor, leaving himself with nothing. Then he sets out to follow Christ, who during his life on earth was unequivocally *incarnated* into the ordinary people, without being thereby insulated from those of other degree. His disciples were first of all fishermen. At Capharnaum he lives in Peter's home. His dealings with the Samaritans, after the conversation by the side of the well, establishes sociologically an absolutely specific *incarnation* into the people. The middle-class world of the synagogue—scribes and Pharisees, and with even more reason the Sadducees—henceforth regard him as alien sociologically. A passage of Luke, the psychological evangelist, stresses this point by means of an extraordinarily profound analysis. Christ had just recounted the parable of the crafty steward, using it to stress the obligation of almsgiving. His concluding words were: "You cannot be the slave both of God and of money." To which the narrative immediately adds: "The Pharisees, who loved money, heard all this and laughed at him." (Lk. 16:1-14).

The psychological content of the passage leaves no room for doubt. Because Christ was *of* the poor, the Pharisees, with their middle-class attitudes, scoff at the exhortatory enthusiasms of the Master in favor of poverty and generosity. Their laughter is in the same category as the remark of the fox that "they are green" in the fable. Besides, St. Paul testifies that Christianity in its origins —without falling into any kind of class conflict—was incarnated in the poor. "Take yourselves, for instance, brothers, at the time you were called: How many of you were wise in the ordinary sense of the word, how many were influential people, or came from noble families? No, it was to shame the wise that God chose what is foolish by human reckoning, and to shame what is strong that he chose what is weak by human reckoning; those whom the world thinks common and contemptible are the ones God has chosen—those who are nothing at all to show up those who are everything. The human race has nothing to boast about to God." (I Co. 1:26–29).

All of this creates a problem for us. Let us take an actual case. A young man of our times goes and sells what he has, giving it to the poor in the form of a transfer of his rights to the religious institution of which he is a member. Then he sets out to follow Christ through his personal incorporation into that institution. The religious institution in question, however, is sociologically *incarnated* into the middle-class strata of society, and in keeping with the norms of that society the religious institution and its members lead a life of poverty by maintaining moderation in their life style—a life style which, nevertheless, is adjusted to middle-class rather than proletarian models—and in particular by observing complete dependence in their use of goods, these all belonging to the institution and not to the members. Even allowing for the less than absolute observance of this formula in practice, it is quite clear that the juridic and ascetic aspects of evangelical poverty are here substantially safeguarded.

Outstanding members of religious orders quite often fulfill them completely and achieve an exceptional level of perfection. Nevertheless, when we turn to the sociological and existential aspect of evangelical poverty, if we compare the extent to which it is realized in modern times (a realization that we have sketched, carrying it to its farthest expression, within the limits of an observant religious life) with what it was in its original state, we see that a radically substantive evolution has occurred. This did not happen, to take an example, in the origins of the Franciscan movement, and that creates a clear apostolic problem and a problem of witness. What must be seen is that the following of Christ is the following of a Messiah whose constitutive and distinctive mark is precisely the evangelization of the poor, while at the same time— as we set out at the beginning—efficacious redemptive action without adequate incarnation is impossible.

Yet another factor in the problem is the self-generating impact of the sociological and existential aspect on the ascetic. A religious poverty carried even to extreme heroism within a community life *incarnated* in middle-class forms and lacking an adequate social projection can hardly suffice to provide a mystique for the religious person in today's world. This does not follow merely from the deeper social sense instilled at the natural level into the younger people, but also to the supernatural social sense that the Holy Spirit has quite clearly breathed into the contemporary Church. The eternal breath of the Spirit today impels us more explicitly in the direction of the dogma of the total Christ (Christ in his Mystical Body) and of the demands of love. From this viewpoint, I believe that the only way to reach a really satisfactory level of practice of evangelical poverty within religious houses is by making the social projection of religious poverty effective, immediate, and visible.

The same comment is valid for self-denial and mortification of the body, virtues that are constantly threatened in our age of highly developed technology, yet most basically connected to the practice of a life of poverty.

To end this short sketch of a subject of inquiry that deserves to be dealt with much more fully, let us look at two solutions and two possible courses of action.

First of all, it is possible to project the social aspect of the vow of poverty into the area of working arrangements of religious institutions with their white-collar and blue-collar employees. That anyone who works for a religious community should exist on a lower living level than the members of that community would seem to me out of line with a proper spirit of evangelical poverty. The fact that such a situation is common among us constitutes in my judgment a relaxation and distortion of that spirit. Why do we not make the decision to live according to the gospel on this point here and now? It is an object of our immediate responsibility. If, in order to do this, we have to sacrifice a part of our standard of living, which may not be very high even now, that may bring into our lives a factor of *incarnation* into the poor of greater import than we suspect, not only because of its causative dynamism in the natural sociological order, but also because of a supernatural dialectic. I believe that if we set out the issues sincerely, the members of our religious communities will be capable —within that formulation of the problem—of greater sacrifices than we had anticipated. And the prophetic value of systematic action in the sense indicated on the part of religious institutions might prove to be nothing less than a principle of salvation for the future of the Church in Spain, a future that today stands gravely compromised. It would even be appropriate to open a channel to the spontaneous generosity of the members in each religious community by giving them the opportunity to surrender benefits voluntarily in order that these be applied immediately to the indicated social purposes. That would facilitate the first steps of an evolution that I suggest is urgent, and that may well have far greater results than may immediately appear.

Another viable solution that might be added to the previous one would be for religious institutes engaged in apostolic or welfare activities to increase the number of jobs set up in a framework of *incarnation*. The means that the member of the institute would share the living standards, the living quarters and the life styles of the poor with whom they are working. Efforts would be made, on this basis, to develop—in addition to the apostolic work—relations of friendship on a level of equality, with mutual understanding, mutual knowledge, confidence, and affection. We members of religious communities frequently have relations of friendship with people at various middle-class levels, but far less commonly with those of lower social strata. It is much harder today for one of the evangelical poor to have a beggar than a banker for his friend. There is no necessary reason why this should be so, and it would not be so if we had in our apostolate as religious a substantial number of activities set up on an unequivocally *incarnational* basis. I already know one such effort. It is still in the formative stage and far from perfect, but it has the qualities that permit one to see the potential of this kind of work. It is the home and chapel of Our Lord of the Well (Nuestro Señor del Pozo) started by Father José Maria de Llanos, S.J., with the approval of his religious and ecclesiastical superiors, in the working-class quarter of Uncle Raymond's Well (Pozo del Tío Raimundo) near the Vallecas Bridge. I mention it simply as an example of a concrete expression of what I am talking about.

Such multiplication, in a serious way and on a substantive rather than a subordinate level, of activities among the poor within a framework of *incarnation*, would have to be supplemented by a strengthening of the bonds of fellowship, affection, and unity among the various work centers of each religious institution (and naturally also between the various religious and priestly institutions). The centers and workshops of religious institutions located

sociologically within the middle-class strata of society would benefit in this way from a lived unity with those *incarnated* in the
working classes. We would thus bring about an effective revitaliza-
tion of religious poverty among ourselves, as an ascetic form, as a
mystique, as an instrument of Christian social progress, and as a
condition for making possible a fruitful apostolate and redemptive
contact of the Church with those poor who ought to be
evangelized.

When I reread this statement sixteen years later, I find it ingenuous on some points and with some elements of a deeper
analysis lacking. Nevertheless, I find it still substantially valid. It
has constituted one of the bases for my later existential reflection
in my search for a true religion.[1]

Some time later I had a letter from a German Jesuit living in
Sweden and attached to the Catholic mission in that country.
This total stranger told me he had read my article and agreed
completely with my views. The problem, he said, was a basic one.
His concluding question, apparently asked without irony, was
whether the cardinals in the Vatican had begun finally to adjust
their thinking along the lines suggested by me.

2. Social Pressures

IN SPAIN and in the Society of Jesus during the 1950s and the
first years of the following decade, the work of anyone whose
conscience had been aroused to a critical analysis of Catholicism
and concretely of the religious situation in Spain found itself
thwarted by structural obstacles maintained by the religious institution itself.

In the spring of 1961, José Maria Gironella published a novel

[1] Because the organizers of that congress omitted it from the proceedings, a
friend had it published in German in the Zurich magazine *Orientierung*,
issue of August 31, 1959. The Spanish text appeared in April 1961, in a
magazine published by the Augustinians, *Religión y Cultura* (religion and culture).

entitled *Un Millón de Muertos*.[2] It provoked a storm of discussion that is hardly imaginable today but that was very real at the time.

The novelist had attempted to deal with the Spanish civil war impartially and primarily in its quality of a human tragedy, avoiding the Manichaean interpretation of a struggle of good against evil.

Spokesmen of the reactionary right launched an attack on Gironella for that specific reason, namely that he did not accept the conventional Manichaean view of the conflict.

Father José M. de Llanos wrote a low-key article in defense of the novel. He thanked the author for helping us to reflect on our past, freeing us from inhuman myths.

I was in Madrid at the time, and I tried to publish an article in a newspaper in support of the Llanos thesis. I was not able to do so because of a prohibition by my superior.

The article had, nevertheless been written with moderation and perhaps even excessive moderation. I had done this deliberately, seeking to avoid any involvement in issues of political conflict by addressing my appeal exclusively to the Christian conscience as such. But the situation of the Christian conscience in Madrid in the year 1961 proved to be a sorry one.

I want to include this hitherto unpublished article here because of the light it sheds on my own spiritual evolution. But the state of my conscience today is more definite and I believe more clearsighted than it was in July 1961. The article was entitled "Above All Earthly Political Considerations."

José Maria Gironella's work, *Un Millón de Muertos*, has given rise to many commentaries, some favorable, others unfavorable. We have even had commentaries on the commentaries. One commentator opposed to the novel and to its defenders offers some words of Pius XII, claiming that they disqualify all views other than his own. This could occasion grave misunderstandings. Quite a number of Catholics were extremely relieved when they read some of the commentaries favorable to Gironella's work,

[2] English title, *One Million Dead* (Garden City, N.Y.: Doubleday, 1963).

34

and these in my opinion had been written with an exemplary evangelical spirit. Such Catholics might now think that the great Pius XII is opposed to the attitude that pleased them. The result might be the development of painful temptations that it is our duty to help to dispel for the simple reason that they lack all foundation.

The words, "Above all earthly political considerations," which serve as title for this article, are taken from Pius XI's talk given at the outset of Spain's warlike conflict (September 14, 1936). At the end of the civil war, Pius XII made a statement on the radio that contained the following important remark: "The sterling Spanish people, with the two characteristic notes of their most noble spirit, which are generosity and frankness, rose up with determination in defense of the ideals of Christian faith and civilization . . . and, helped by God, succeeded in resisting the attacks of those who, deceived by what they believed to be a humanitarian ideal of raising up the lowly, in reality were fighting only for the benefit of atheism." The two talks of Pius XI and Pius XII are pastoral exhortations, the one of sympathy, the other of congratulation. They make no claim to decide questions of doctrine, and they leave standing the freedom of Catholics to judge a very complex historical event, one fraught with earthly political aspects, some of which may even be contradictory.

In addition, the personal attitude of both Pius XI and Pius XII is full of admirable balance. Both state in express terms that a religious persecution of unusual virulence had been unloosed in Spain (at the root of which were anti-Christian ideologies and the action of destructive forces) and that there has been a very big number of victims (priests, religious, and lay people) sacrificed through hatred of religion and granted by God the grace of martyrs to enable them to die nobly and religiously. I do not think that Gironella denies or hides any of that, and still less the members of religious orders who have commented on his novel. But this does not prejudge in any way regarding the weight of the responsibility on one side and the other for the chain of factors that drew us to the catastrophe of the civil war.

Worthy of reflection is the statement of Pius XII that those who in fact fought for the benefit of atheism did so because they were "deceived by what they believed to be a humanitarian ideal of raising up the lowly." The great Pope here recognizes clearly that men of good faith were to be found in the ranks of the adversaries. Why did they deceive themselves? Was the fault entirely theirs, or even principally theirs? Only God can give the final answer when his time comes. The stand of Pius XI is therefore a beautiful and a Christian one: "We cannot for a moment doubt what we must do: to love them with a special love which unites compassion and mercy; to love them and pray for them, so that they may dispassionately recognize the truth and so that their hearts may reopen to seek the true good and join as brothers in pursuing it."

Twenty-five years later, I believe we can expand in humility the prayer of Pope Pius XII. We can ask for ourselves that our hearts may be truly opened to this desire of the true good and this brotherly pursuit of it.

Much stress has been placed on Gironella's efforts to present the civil war as an enormous evil that we should recall with sorrow, and some commentators were severely critical of those who praised that aspect of the novel. I respect the different viewpoints, but I think these stirring and appropriate words of Pius XI may help to clarify the matter: "And over the tumult and this unbridled violence, across the burnings and the slaughter, a voice announces to the world the start of a civil war between the children of the same country, the same community, the same fatherland. My God! War is always—even in theory—sad, dreadful, and inhuman. One man looks for another so that he can kill him, so that he can kill the greatest possible number of his own kind, to do them harm by ever more deadly means. It has been said that blood shed by a brother is blood to the end of time."

May God free us from such dreadful and long-lasting hatreds.

3. The Christian Conscience and Marxism

FOR ME THE STUDY of Marx and of Marxism-Leninism in some depth was a professional obligation.

I have not become an expert in Marxism, but I do know something about it, and my reflection as a Christian has been helped by it.

The study of Marx led me to the study of the "master-slave

dialectic," as formulated in Hegel's *Phenomenology of the Spirit*. This study, combined with meditation on the way Marx inverted this dialectic of Hegel, passing from a supposed dialectic justification of slavery to a dialectic justification of liberation, forced me to think deeply.

In the light of the counterbalancing positions of Hegel and Marx, I rethought what might be called the essence of Christianity as a lived life, in human history and human society.

But this brought me to recognize that Christianity as lived life has not yet come to pass. Christians as they exist historically do not live their Christianity. The analysis that Karl Marx makes of religion as "the opium of the people," a structural obstacle to man's liberation, an "ideology" sustained by and sustaining a social situation of structural oppression and injustice (with a powerful economic dimension) is valid for an enormous percentage (we might say for 80 percent) of the religion we Christians live as Christianity, but which in reality is many other things.

All of this has exercised a major impact on the maturing of my faith, as today I live it.

An early result of my reflections on Hegel, Marx, and Christianity was a paper I presented in Madrid to a philosophy week toward the end of the 1950s. The text was published in the *Revista de Filosofía* (review of philosophy), Madrid, January–February 1962.

This short text is essential for any explanation of the maturing of my awareness, not as the final goal, but as a starting point. For that reason, I include it here. It was entitled "Three Constitutive Attitudes of the Person in His Social Relationships."

There is a page in Hegel's *Phenomenology of the Spirit* that is today particularly pertinent. It is where he describes the dialectic of "master" and "slave."[3] For Hegel the *moment* of independence that is essential for the person as a person (the "being in himself" and the "being for himself") can occur only in the

[3] G. W. F. Hegel, *Phänomenologie des Geistes*. Selbstbewusstsein, A. Herrschaft und Knechtschaft. Lasson edition, pp. 146–50.

struggle of two counterpoised consciousnesses. A person's own consciousness faces up to an alien, strange, and hostile consciousness. A struggle is inevitable, and it must be a struggle to the death, in order that the consciousness may reach its dialectical unfolding as a "self-consciousness," a personal consciousness ("in itself" and "for itself"). This takes place by means of the dialectic of the "master" and the "slave." The human consciousness is in itself a dialectic of nature (contingency, particularity, dependence) and of personhood (absolute substantivity, universality of the pure "being for itself"). In order to affirm the *moment* of personhood, it is necessary to deny dialectically the *moment* of nature. This dialectic negation occurs because, in the struggle of the two hostile consciousnesses, one is dominant and the other subject. The dominant consciousness (the "master") prefers freedom over life and is ready to die. In this way he brings about the dialectic negation of the *moment* of nature and proclaims himself to be a "personal self-consciousness," but without disappearing in the effort, thanks to the fact that the other consciousness (the "slave") has *feared* (dialectically, radical) death and has given in in order to save his *moment* of nature (his reality, his natural being), accepting slavery in order not to perish and thus avoiding the consummation of the struggle to the death in an absolute and inert negativeness, a conclusion that does not fit into the constitutively dialectic unfolding of the consciousness, which in the last instance is the Absolute Spirit. But the dialectic movement continues inexorably. The antithetical negation represented by the slave consciousness is overcome (*aufgehoben*) in a "mediation" (*Aufhebung*), in which the absolute self-affirmation of the "master" becomes *alienation* (the master *depends* on the slave, is enslaved to the slave, and at the same time his strictly absurd enjoyment of the slave's work disintegrates into a maximum of contingent fluidity, of *negativity*), while the *alienation* of the "slave" becomes a *reaffirmation* (recognition) of his personal *moment*, expressed in *creative work*, as a result of which the slave detaches himself from nature and rises above contingency. This reciprocal dialectic *mediation* of "master" and "slave" becomes *reconciliation* (*Versöhnung*) in the mutual recognition of "master" and "slave" as persons (a recognition in which each consciousness affirms *itself* as a person *in the other*).

For the outsider this page of Hegel may seem nothing more than a vacantly abstract philosophic "game." Nothing could be farther from the reality. The thought of Hegel is, in itself, a continuous dialectic of abstraction and concretization, of unusually limited conceptual imagining, and of accurate existential conception.

Hegel represents vitally in himself the spirit of the genial middle class which, in the years following the philosopher's death, carried out the modern capitalist revolution. His dialectic of "master" and "slave," abstract as it may appear, gives us a master key to an understanding of the *spirit of capitalism*, a spirit that unfortunately has not been essentially overcome in the West. The existence of a radically dominant *class* (the "master") and of a servant *class* (the "slave") appears to be justified as an essential condition without which the highest values of the spirit could not be realized. The injustice of slavery is thus disguised in the *holiness* of the spirit. In addition, struggle and warfare are canonized in their own right under the form of "a gentlemen's war" at the expense of the "slaves." But the "slave" will never be able to rise up and fight his "master," because his role is that of surrender and servitude. It is true that Hegel hints at a *reconciliation*, at a mutual recognition of the "master" and the "slave," as persons. But this reconciliation is far from being *authentic*. It is an unincarnated and abstract (inoperative) recognition, for which Hegel regards stoicism as the model. It leaves untouched the injustices and the consequent *alienations* of the "master" (who seeks a compromise that will free him from the risk of rebellion by the "slave" and ensure his position as dominator, and that is not compatible with a real and concrete recognition of the *person* of the "slave") and also those of the "slave" (prevented by his "slavery" from authentically living his "creative" work in which he would be able to "re-create" himself). The fact that in other historic circumstances, or in exceptional cases, very different kind of relations between masters and servants may have been possible in no way lessens the reality of the relations created by capitalism, which has its root in the bourgeois spirit as revealed for us by Hegel, as long ago as 1807, in its deepest and most secret essence.

Marx surmised the real and realistic meaning of Hegel's dialectic of the "master" and the "slave" in his *Economic and Philosophical Manuscripts* of 1844, published in Volume 3, Section 1, of Rjazanov's critical edition of the works of Marx and Engels.[4]

[4] Karl Marx und Friedrich Engels: *Historisch-Kristische Gesamtausgabe*, edited by D. Rjazanov, Vol. 3, Section 1 (especially pp. 82–94).

Marx agreed with Hegel's dialectical formulation of the issue, but he believed that the terms of the dialectic development should be inverted. The starting point is not the struggle, but rather the (peaceful) work that effects the unity of man with nature and of man with man. At this point, however, the totalitarian character of Marx's way of seeing things—a character also derived from Hegel—comes into play. The notion of man's unity with nature is ambiguous in Marx, because the *moment* of independence is not sufficiently safeguarded, and the radical originality of the spirit is sadly sacrificed. The union of man with man is brought about at the expense of the real person, who is deprived of a transcendental destiny, of an authentic personal substantivity, of a genuine *moment* of spiritual freedom, being reduced instead to being absorbed in *generic* man. Marx conceives this generic man as a "concrete general entity" in a realist-materialist version (in the dialectic sense), yet one who, with regard to the *person* of each man, turns out—paradoxically—to be no more than an abstraction, to which are sacrificed the real persons (the "sons of man" who are simultaneously "sons of God").

How is the step from the *moment* of work (unity) to the *moment* of mortal struggle taken? Marx sees it as taken by reason of an unjust seizure of the fruits of work by the "masters," which is at the very center of capitalist property (private ownership of capital and *purchase* of the work force), and by means of which the worker is violently separated from (dispossessed of) the natural fruit of his work, which becomes for him an instrument of *alienation*. This alienation can be overcome (*aufgehoben*) only by means of the revolution (the "mortal struggle") which, by suppressing the *oppressor class*, restores the original unity by achieving the reconciliation (*Versöhnung*) of man with nature and of man with man.

This concept of Marx also proves to be inadmissible because of its totalitarianism (tied to an entirely materialist-historic outlook, essentially atheistic) and because of its *radical* constitutive *violence* (the mortal struggle of the classes is a "dialectical mediation [*Aufhebung*]," which is not only inevitable *de facto*, but which is constitutively *de jure*; it is a *constitutive moment* of the immanent dialectic of history). A comparison of Marx and Hegel, nevertheless, establishes the fact that the fundamentality of the "struggle" and of the "hatred" is more radical in Hegel than in Marx. The initial *moment* of Marx, peaceful and harmonious work, is better than that of Hegel, which is hostility and "mortal struggle." This remains true in spite of the totalitarian overtone —which is certainly inadmissible, but which in any case equally affect's Hegel's view. As for Marx's atheism (which is a materialist-dialectic pantheism), it also is quite close to the idealistic monism of Hegel. One might say that, in comparison with Hegel, Marx was justified up to a certain point; but only in comparison with Hegel, because—objectively speaking—Marx's starting point is not only inadequate but substantively false.

The true starting point, the original attitude of social intercourse that gives its root meaning to the existence of the human person, is set out for us in one of the original monuments of the human spirit, a document that is in addition, for the believer, inspired by God. I am referring to Genesis, and specifically to that part of it that represents the oldest cycle of traditions. There we find the account of the making of Eve and of her encounter with Adam. In this story we have a really striking combination of cultural infantility and human profundity, a profundity that is truly metaphysical in the best sense of that word. "It is not good that the man should be alone," Yahweh said (Gn. 2:18). By the work of God the man falls into a profound sleep. From his rib is formed a woman whom God brings to Adam. And Adam, whom the theory of all the animals of creation had left unmoved, now wakes up and recognizes himself in the woman, his other *I*, his "I in the other." He breaks out in an exclamation by means of which he expresses the deepest recesses of his existence, of his being as a person: "This at last is bone from my bones and flesh from my flesh!" (Gn. 2:19–23).

The Genesis account places us on the right road. Man does not establish himself adequately in his personal being without *the other*. Man sleeps. The encounter in which he awakes to recognize himself in the *you* is the encounter of love. The other is not *hostile*, not even strange, but rather *my other I*, my *I in the other*. The love through which man encounters himself in *the other* simultaneously distinguishes him from nature, making him a person. The *I* and the *you* ("my you") exist in a unity, not, however, in the unity of generic man but in that of an *open interpersonal communion*. The discovery of the *you*, which is the revelation of the *I*, is presented in Genesis in what is undoubtedly the most profound as well as the most charming and appealing episode of all world literature. Conjugal love is, at the same time, simply the most radical and primary concretization of a loving dialectic of *encounter* and recognition, which is open (open without limits) to levels of realization distinct from that of the erotic love, which is proper to conjugal *eros*. The unlimited nature of the opening, which is proper to the authentic love to which man is called from the beginning, ensures true, real, and concrete universality. It is the "concrete universal," which for Hegel and even for Marx had been dissolved, alienated in pure abstraction. Man without love, in his egoistic loneliness, is *alienated*. He is submerged in the primitive stupor out of which only love can lift him.

The affirmation that man establishes himself adequately in his personal being through the medium of his loving encounter with the *you* has a strict philosophic value. It does not mean that the man who does not love (in an authentic and *interpersonal* way) is purely and simply not a human person. He is a human person, but not in an authentic and complete way. His *personality* is non-human (it has not been "constituted" in the true sense). His personality is *alienated*.

Love is not an accidental calling of the person into action, but an *existential act* through which the innermost essence of man becomes fully constituted. The essence of man, as essence, is not fully actualized without love. It does not fulfill its deepest need. It is not authentically itself. It is *alienated*.

How is it possible to demonstrate that love is truly the metaphysical destiny through which man as a person is constituted? Admittedly, this cannot be demonstrated by an abstract dialectic of concepts. What we are dealing with here is a radical experience of a simultaneously existential and metaphysical nature. It is an experience in which love constitutes us adequately as *persons*, giving us an authentically *personal* consciousness. As St. Augustine puts it: "Give me a lover, and he will understand what I am saying. . . . But if I speak to one who lacks passion, he won't know what I am talking about."[5]

The starting point, therefore, is neither the struggle of Hegel nor the nature-style unity of Marx (Adam asleep among the animals in Paradise). The starting point is the authentic and open

[5] St. Augustine: In Joannis Evangelium, Tract 26, on the words "No one can come to me . . ." (Jn. 6:44). (*Da amantem, et sentit quod dico . . . si autem frigido loquor, nescit quid loquor.*)

love in which a true personal consciousness is created. This is the open love that is *fruitful, multiplies, and fills the earth* (see Gn. 1:28). It is this love alone that makes work *human*. Man constitutes himself authentically a *person* in love. And because love is creative, man works *humanly*, creatively. In Genesis man works for the woman who is with child. The starting point is the original conciliation of love. The *alienation* of man is the denial of love (a denial that is more radical in the Hegelian "master" than in the Marxist "proletarian" who *hates* his exploiter, because hate incorporates a perverted kind of interpersonal *recognition*, which is absent from absolute, existential nonrecognition). *Reconciliation* is brought about only in love. This is, however, not a Platonic form of love but a love that is authentically *incarnated*; a love that expresses itself in deeds (here is inserted the *moment* of work) and works justice, because it recognizes the *you* in its full dignity as a person, thus recognizing itself through love in *the other* and *the other* in itself.

These then are the three constitutive attitudes of the person in human social intercourse proposed respectively by Hegel, by Marx, and by the Judeo-Christian tradition.

A final question of particular importance remains. As regards the point just discussed, Marx represents an improvement on Hegel, which cannot in turn be improved on by Hegel. It is quite clear that Hegel represents very accurately the spiritual roots of nineteenth-century capitalism. The capitalism of today has admittedly evolved significantly in the democratic countries of high economic development. But it is obvious that the progress did not come from a further growth from the roots that were exposed in the Hegelian dialectic of "master" and "slave." Rather it came from a compromise with pressures produced by the class struggle (once again placing Marx closer to the truth than Hegel), a struggle that—one might add—has proved to be far more complex than the dialectic "model" of Marx represented it to be. In the dialectic tension that today places communism in opposition to capitalism, the only possible authentic *mediation* is *reconciliation* in love in work and in truth (*opere et veritate*), a love that works justice. But perhaps the day of the great metanoia, the day of the great change of heart, is still distant. The world may still have to be cleansed in the fires of even greater suffering. Be that as it may, the task of the true "children of light," wherever they may be found, is to work with love under the sign of hope.

When I reread this text after an interval of more than a decade, its viewpoints still seem to me to be fundamentally valid. It represented a very important stage in the process of clarification of my conscience as a Christian.

It was my first intuitive awareness that capitalism is not merely an economic technique, neutral from the humanist perspective, much less a necessity inscribed in the nature of things to be identified and analyzed by "science," but on the contrary the result of the will to exploit, of a strategy of exploitation, of oppressing violence, and of a structure of mechanisms of exploitation. This intuition has been for me irreversible. I am indebted for it to Hegel. Thanks to his genial insight I have had exposed for me, for all time, the intimate structure of the phenomenon of bourgeois capitalism and of all the voyages of socio-economic exploitation that had preceded it.

It was my realization that we have to say "no" to exploitation and to the *structures* of exploitation. For this realization I am indebted to Karl Marx. As for the Catholic mentality of the 1950s, far from helping me to understand this truth, it was a solid obstacle blocking the way.

Once I understood that I had to say "no" to exploitation, and that of course not only verbally but with appropriate positive actions, my Christian reflection forced me to move forward on a new road. I found myself face to face—in previously unsuspected terms—with the problem of true and false religion.

Together with these positive aspects, which are permanently valid, I now recognize that my analysis in "Three Constitutive Attitudes of the Person in His Social Relationships" has certain limitations, which I was subsequently able to overcome.

The first is an unduly simplistic and hurried discrediting of Marx on philosophic grounds. The fact that Marx's philosophy (materialist immanentism) is not mine, and that in consequence his anthropology is not mine, does not authorize me to rush ahead so precipitously to rejecting it on the grounds of inescapable totalitarianism.

44

The one-sided stress on the person as a social product, does not —in good Marxism—necessarily exclude admitting that the personal subject may dialectically represent a *moment* of irreducible originality that it is necessary to respect. Nevertheless, it is obvious that this stress, when combined with the denial of a transcendence in the strict sense of the human person (what we Christians call "the image of God"), carries with it an intrinsic danger of falling into totalitarianism.

But we Christians, who have lived and who continue to live in our own flesh all that weight of totalitarianism that is permitted on top of the transcendence we proclaim (even at times to the point of smothering it), should not protest too much the dangers of totalitarian deviation inherent in an immanentist anthropology.

The problem of not yielding to the temptation of totalitarian power is one we all share. We should be very concerned about it. But we cannot write Marx off without a thought as inescapably totalitarian, when he sets out to free all the oppressed from all that oppresses them. And less than to anyone else is this permissible to socially conservative Catholics, who—whether they are aware of it or not—are accepting the dialectic of "master" and "slave."

Another limitation of my essay is the unduly summary disqualification of class warfare as understood by Marx. The fact is that Marx (unlike Engels) conceives of the dialectic rather as rigorously historical than as quasimetaphysical. What is necessarily at issue is not a root violence but rather a violence imposed by the violence of the "master" and intended to suppress violence ("the classless society"). But the problem of the violence of the "master" and the need of class warfare to put an end to it is one attached to the basic web of history. In the reality of history it is truly a key point. In consequence, it is a dialectic necessity.

It took seven or eight years for me to clear up these points for myself by reflecting and meditating on them, thus finally freeing myself from the residue of ideological anti-Marxism that had carried over from the conservative Catholic tradition in which I had been trained.

45

I set out my definitive stand on the issue of class warfare in a lecture I gave in Oviedo on October 8, 1970:

Some would like to get away from the issue once for all by asserting that in today's neocapitalist society the notion of "class" has lost all meaning. It is true that a rigidly dichotomous concept of "middle class" and of "proletariat" cannot be longer held. But to jump from this to the claim that no "classes" exist and that consequently there cannot be "discrimination" between classes is to fly over a chasm. A source that is free of any suspicion of Marxism, the *Staatlexikon* published by Herder, in its article entitled *Klasse* by F. A. Hermens (Vol. 4, 1959, col. 1062 ff.), gives a description of social "class" that is highly pertinent. Unlike social "groups" (which are differentiations that can exist, among themselves, in a horizontal relationship), "classes" are strata or layers with an order of social superiority and inferiority (a "vertical" relationship from above to below). The community of class (and the class "condition") affects the entire family, not just the individual. A difference of class is expressed by external signs of discrimination. For example, marriage and shared living (*connubium et convivium*) of members of different classes are impossible in practice. Behind this lies a whole system of customs, attitudes, and material interests. Ownership (the property system) and privilege play an important part in the consolidation of "classes."

It would not be easy to list the classes and spell out precisely the point at which one shades into another. Opportunity for passing from one class to another may have increased somewhat. But the fact of "classes," in the descriptive sense, is obvious. And it is also clear that classes of this kind suppose the existence of discrimination. (Race discrimination in multiracial countries is only one kind, more easily seen than some others.) It is further clear that Vatican Council II, in its Constitution on the Church in the Modern World (No. 29), calls for the elimination of every type of discrimination affecting the basic rights of the person, whether in the social or cultural field, by reason of race, or because of "social condition" (which is to say, because of "class"). It also urged the elimination of class discriminations of a cultural character (No. 60); of class discriminations in conditions of work and pay (No. 66); and of class discriminations of a political nature (No. 75). It regards excessive economic differences as constituting an element of "discrimination" ("They are contrary to social justice, to equity, to the dignity of the human person, as well as to social and international peace." No. 29).

All of this brings out clearly the extreme ambiguity of presenting "class collaboration" as a Christian ideal. Class collaboration assumes acceptance of a system of highly discriminatory classes. That is not the Christian ideal. The Christian ideal is a classless society, which does not mean a uniform society. What it means is a society in which, instead of "classes," there are only functional social "groups," the differences between them being nondiscriminatory (they are maintained substantially on a horizontal line and are not based on privilege). This is a guiding ideal toward which we must strive to move in all seriousness. To accept this guiding ideal calls for a structural revolution in our middle-class capitalist societies. (In the socialist societies new "class" contradictions can arise, and it will be necessary to fight to eliminate them. In actual fact, nevertheless, as regards the problem of elimination of class discriminations, I believe that the socialist societies represent a decided progress. To see this, one has only to read as independent a novel as Aleksandr I. Solzhenitsyn's *Cancer Ward*).

If, then, our objective is to move as effectively as possible from our liberal, bourgeois, capitalist society firmly structured in support of class discrimination, to a society that will come close to the ideal of a classless society, can this be done without a struggle, if not in arms, at least energetic and extending to the whole of cultural, civil, and social life? And if such a struggle is necessary, what are the social factors of our world as it is now structured on which we will have to count to effect it? Can we expect the backing of the privileged and upper classes, or only that of the lower classes, which are the victims of the discrimination? Welcome indeed to every element that is willing to join in the struggle for a classless society (a society without class discriminations). But who can reasonably doubt that such a struggle, when it becomes a concrete and practical issue, is going to be a struggle of the exploited and dominated classes (together with all who may join them) against the privileged classes who, as a group, defend their privileges (and we all can see with our own eyes how much force and violence they use).

The great Christian principle is neither the class struggle nor "interclass" collaboration. The Christian principle is love of one's neighbor, including one's enemy, and a hunger for justice, because love does not act unjustly (see Rm. 13:10).

In a society of discriminatory classes, the class struggle (carried on by the oppressed classes) to overcome the discriminations and move toward a society without classes is not contrary to Christianity. Of course, for the man who follows the great principle of love of his neighbor, this guiding principle affects his approach to the struggle also. But it does not exclude an attitude of struggle. Quite the contrary. The principle of love drives a man to seek justice ardently and to hate the structural factors favoring injustice.

What is contrary to Christianity is the resistance on the part of the "privileged" classes to the establishment of a society without discriminations (of a society without "classes").

In the letter of James (1:9-10), the suggestion seems to be made that the rich Christian, if he is truly a Christian, wishes to be stripped of his socially privileged status because it proves, from the viewpoint of the Gospel, to be something negative. Or, as St. James puts it: "It is right for the poor brother to be proud of his high rank, and the rich one to be thankful that he has been humbled, because riches last no longer than the flowers in the grass; the scorching sun comes up, and the grass withers, the flower falls; what looked so beautiful now disappears. It is the same with the rich man: His business goes on; he himself perishes." In this text, it seems clear that the "pride" of the poor brother is represented as a positive value that results from the fact of being "poor" (not "rich" or socially "privileged"), when the reality is seen from the perspective of the Gospel. The "humble condition" is, in evangelical terms, an "uplifting." The reason is that the poor are the object of God's choice, as St. James insists in the same Letter: "It was those who are poor according to the world that God chose, to be rich in faith and to be the heirs to the kingdom which he promised to those who love him." (Jm. 2:5).

It is appropriate to ask what is the "humiliation" for which the rich man should be "thankful" in the thinking of St. James. It is obvious that he should not be thankful that, because he is rich, he is in an unfavorable position with respect to the Gospel. Rather is it because of his recognition (and joyful acceptance) of the fact that riches are transitory ("because riches last no longer than the flowers in the grass"). It is because of his hope of seeing himself "freed" from his riches because of their transitoriness. That may seem ridiculous. But it is precisely what the New Testament says in the passage just cited from St. James. What this means is that a true Christian belonging to a higher class in a class-dominated society will sincerely wish to see a social transformation into a classless society in which his "high rank" will wither away. Unfortunately, few rich Christians are prepared "to be thankful that [they have] been humbled" in the sense in which St. James says they should be.

Another aspect of my study, "Three Constitutive Attitudes of the Person in His Social Relationships," which has stood the test of time, is the centrality and fundamentality of open interpersonal love, of agape (not a closed egoism of two or of a group but open interpersonal communion). I would merely clarify that this love, in which in very truth "salvation" is found, must not be misunderstood, as we Christians have often misunderstood it. It has absolutely no relationship with the bland conformism that would of necessity transform the religion of love into "the opium of the people." Christian love, which is the message of Jesus, establishes a dialectic of love and justice, of interaction between the microsocial sphere of primary interpersonal relations and the macrosocial (political) sphere of community of interests and responsibilities at the level of mankind in general.

Hegel helped me to understand Marx. Marx brought me to the rediscovery of Jesus Christ and the meaning of his message. Jesus and his message have forced me to recognize that we Christians are not Christians, and that the Catholic Church as it exists in history has little about it that is Christian. I feel, in consequence, called to penance, to change of heart, and to reconstruction.

In Hegel I recognize a wise man, perhaps a grandson of Lamech (see Gn. 4:23–24). In Marx I recognize a prophet, a unique offshoot of Amos, Jeremiah, and Zephaniah, the messianic prophet of "the classless society" (Ws. 3:11–13).

Jesus is the Son of God, the Christ in whom I believe.

Marx's teaching, which can never constitute a dogma either for the authentic Christian or the genuine Marxist, is located on the plane of political, socio-economic, and historical analysis. Jesus lives for the believer on the plane of faith and love (agape), of open love with all its dynamisms.

49

Christianity cannot be converted into a political instrument of Marxist socialism. But neither can it be converted into a political instrument of "anticommunism." And that, nevertheless, has occurred. It has occurred extensively, in fact to the point where the religion of Christians—as lived and operative in history—became rather the opium of the people and an instrument of their oppression and of injustice than the other way around.

For a number of years, I have striven with every means at my disposal to win back for Christians the freedom of conscience that is their right, so that they might be able to make their own choices in a world in which injustices and situations of oppression cry out to God.

Acceptance of the Marxist analysis of history, and of such elements as the historic meaning of class struggle and the need to get away from private ownership of the means of production, is in no way contrary to the faith or to the Gospel.

The Christian inspiration of the believer who faces up to his human, historical, and political responsibilities means to love his neighbor as himself. It means a personal liberation from greed and egoism, with the corresponding commitment to community, a respect for the dignity of every man as a person, and a relentless opposition to oppression of the weak—that is to say, a biblical sense of justice.

These principles in Christianity are not doctrinal ones, and still less political. They are prophetic principles, to be lived by each in his own life. The duty of the Christian is to try to be at the service of these principles as best he can, and particularly to avoid betraying them in his life, in his actions, and in his relations with the world. How is this to be done? Let each of us respect the liberty of the Christian conscience of others. Among ourselves as Christians, let us recognize a plurality of political options, as is normal and absolutely necessary between members of the same Christian church. The unity of Christians is unity in faith in Jesus Christ and acceptance of the Gospel as "prophecy." It is not a political unity.

The fact is that, in the present condition of the world, a growing number of Christians are coming to the conclusion that it is their duty to make common cause with all who are committed to socialism in the cause of revolution. The objective conditions of historic society are such that it would be a serious sin against the Gospel to try to prevent such Christians from making their choice on this issue in accord with the freely determined dictate of their conscience.

For two hundred years, the Catholic community and its structures of power and culture have tried, in the name of the faith, to prevent every revolutionary change of structures. This shocking fact has, since Pope John XXIII and the Second Vatican Council, begun to lose its monolithic quality. But the change is taking place slowly, and with many hesitations, which reveal the strength of the reactionary forces that still survive.

Mechanisms of oppression and injustice continue to be maintained, consciously or unconsciously, under the cloak of Christianity. And vested interests are being protected.

This is still happening, in spite of the warning given from the very beginning to Christians against such a danger, in the Letter of James (2:1): "My brothers, do not try to combine faith in Jesus Christ, our glorified Lord, with the making of distinctions between classes of people."

4. True Religion and False Religion

AFTER MANY YEARS of reflection and of a life lived within Christianity as it historically exists, I have come to see where the difference between true and false religion lies.

When Marx says that religion is the opium of the people (an obstacle to the freeing of man from unjust oppression, an instrument of injustice at the service of the oppressor system), his statement is more profound and more accurate than Catholics usually imagine.

51

A first reply to the Marxian accusation is that the criticism may be justifiable in the case of some false religions, but not in the case of Christianity, the true religion.

Such an answer is superficial. Taken as a whole, Catholicism for the past two centuries has been far more an obstacle to freedom and an instrument of oppression than the other way about.

As regards this issue, I have succeeded in reaching a very clear stand. The results of my study, my reflection, and the experience provided by my own life were all put together in a talk I gave in Oviedo on October 7, 1970:

The Church has been guilty of a great social and historical sin in the past two centuries by its uncritical acceptance of and cooperation with the modern capitalist system, a system that reflects an antichristian concept of man and society and that has created an excessively unjust society. In its dealings with that society the Church has been and continues to be unduly conservative.

The concept of man and society underlying modern capitalism comes from the Enlightenment. The eighteenth century saw a true cultural revolution known as "secularization" and "enlightenment." These are two aspects of a single phenomenon: a recognition by science and philosophy of their autonomy vis-à-vis theology, and an attempt to provide a rational (and systematic) explanation of world reality. This cultural revolution was in part very positive. But it was also in part negative.

What is here pertinent is that this new philosophy of the Enlightenment carried with it a new vision of social reality that was heavily laden with historic consequences.

It is clear, of course, that the concept of man and society developed by the Enlightenment rationalism of the eighteenth century had earlier historic roots. Cultural roots are to be found in the individualism that was stressed by the Scholastic nominalism of the late Middle Ages and in the *ethos* of affirmation of the individual developed during the Renaissance. Socio-economic roots went back to the commercial revolution brought about by the Crusades and the resultant birth of mercantile and financial capitalism, especially in the Italian republics, as Europe was passing from the Middle Ages into the modern era.

The rediscovery of the worth of the individual was in itself positive. This occurred, however, not in a *personalist* framework but in an *individualist* one. That distinction has been developed discerningly by Erich Fromm in *Escape from Freedom* (New York: Holt, Rinehart & Winston, 1941), a book that combines solid psychological insights with data drawn from deep historical analysis.

The medieval manner of inserting man into society corresponded to an *infantile* attitude of identification of the self with the surrounding world. The awakening of individuality, characteristic of the passage to the modern era, would correspond to what in the development of the child constitutes the crisis of adolescence. But this adolescent character means that this kind of affirmation of the individual lacks the balance proper to authentic personality (which reaffirms the liberty and responsibility of the I in openness to the you and to the us, to dialogue and to love). It occurs rather in terms of an individualism which incorporates elements of narcissism and of sadomasochism. It is locked into itself (egoism) and related to the "other" in terms of competition, acute jealousy, a desire to dominate, or an unconditional surrender to the leader.

Eighteenth-century rationalist philosophy built its concept of man and society on this foundation of individualism. To summarize as much as possible while retaining the essential elements, that concept may be described as follows:

1. It accepted man's radical selfishness not as a sin against which one must fight, but as the very law of nature, which must be respected. A man should be radically selfish and should operate accordingly. The only thing this concept (cast in an individualistic and rationalist mold) demands of man is that his selfishness should be rigorously rational and highly intelligent.

2. An effort to recover to some extent the old notion of a common good (which had been destroyed). The effort followed a strange course and was conditioned in part by the spectacular progress made during the eighteenth century by the physical and mathematical sciences. This progress led to the tendency to conceive the common good in mechanistic terms.

The effort to recover the concept of a common good by means of a mechanistic model is based on the following assumption. If in the course of social relations, each individual follows his selfish interests cold-bloodedly with complete disregard for all others, but

I BELIEVE IN HOPE

in an intelligent way, a balance of all these selfish interests and efforts will occur objectively, by means of a kind of self-regulating social mechanism. This will finally lead to the common good, or at least to the greatest possible common good, and consequently to the true common good, the real common good.

This assumption underlies the economic theory of the classic economists (Adam Smith), as well as the theory of Rousseau's social contract. It similarly underlies the society built by and on modern capitalism. The structures of the capitalist world respond to this philosophy and strengthen it.

The historic sin of nineteenth-century Christianity is that it accepted the social and economic philosophy of capitalism (it accepted it in practice), while simultaneously rejecting the positive elements of political liberalism. This acceptance of the presuppositions of capitalism grew stronger after 1848, as a result of the totally negative reaction of the Christians of that period (with few exceptions) to the socialist revolution. The excessively monolithic and uncritical opposition to the historic phenomenon of modern socialism is another aspect of the nineteenth-century Church's historic and social sin, and even today it continues to constitute a heavy liability.

One is, nevertheless, forced to ask how nineteenth-century Christians could accept a view of society based on the admission of radical selfishness and an equilibrium of selfish interests, when love, brotherhood, a community of hearts and goods, a sense of fellowship and of social justice are the very essence of Christianity.

Considerable light has been thrown on the problem by theologian Johannes B. Metz in "The Church's Social Function in the Light of a Political Theology."[6]

The contradiction between Christianity and the egoistic concept of man and of society is so obvious that Christians had to create a device which would permit them to accept the social philosophy of capitalism. They made a distinction between the area of macrosocial relations and that of microsocial (family, etc.). All this was done unconsciously, implicitly, and tacitly. At the macrosocial level of socio-economic relations appropriate to the industrial era and to the economy of an objectivized and universalized market, Christians accepted uncritically (and selfishly) the liberal economic concept of the market of selfish interests.

[6] *Faith and the World of Politics*, Concilium series, Johannes B. Metz, ed. (New York: Paulist Press, 1968), Vol. 36, pp. 2–18.

Meanwhile, Christian values were reserved for the Christian family, for the personal and strictly private area of relations. In this way, Christians also failed to see that the possibilities of truly living the Christian evangelical values at the family and private level are conditioned by the need to affirm the principles of community and mutual support at the social level. The fact is that the man who accepts the philosophy of egoism at the macrosocial level cannot claim to live according to the Gospel at the microsocial level. Christian love cannot be confined to the personal and family sphere.

Very serious consequences followed at the level of economic and social structures from this acceptance by nineteenth-century Christianity of the liberal capitalist world-view. The first was an almost total failure to recognize the injustices of capitalism. (The extent of this lack of awareness is clearly established by the careful study of the problem of the just wage made by James Healy in an important book, *The Just Wage, 1750–1890: A Study of Moralists from St. Alphonsus to Leo XIII* [The Hague: Martinus Nijhoff, 1966].) There was, further, the failure to understand the efforts of such Catholics as Jean-Marie Lamennais and Frederic Ozanam to lead the Christian community out of its state of social sin, as well as the radical lack of understanding of the reasons for and positive values of the socialist revolution.

Here we have a very serious problem for the believing Christian.

If true religion is not and cannot be an instrument of injustice in the world, and if at the same time the religion of Christians (and concretely that of Catholics) has been and continues to be (taken as a whole, and on balance) a factor tending to maintain structures of oppression and injustice, then the conclusion inescapably follows that the religion that Catholics live is not the true religion.

It is a complex problem for one like me, a believer in Jesus Christ with the absolute commitment of the "yes" of faith.

I say this because the religion that Catholics live has its center in faith in Jesus Christ. To what extent it is a genuine faith, deserving to be called faith, God will judge by his own definitive decision in each case.

How can a religious way of living, centered on faith in Jesus Christ, who is the living truth, turn out to be a false religion?

I have been helped in my search for the answer by my study of and faith-guided meditation on the Bible, by examining the social ideas of the Fathers of the Church, from the so-called Apostolic Fathers to St. Gregory the Great (in the middle of the sixth century), and also by going as deeply as my circumstances permitted into the history of religions.

Religion falls into one of two types. It is either ontological-cultist or ethicoprophetic. The first type is found in its purest form in the "mystery" religions that flourished in the world of Greece and Asia Minor in the Greco-Roman period.

This type of religion corresponds to a circular concept of history. History repeats itself (as in nature, the cycle of the seasons). There is no real progress, no sense of history moving toward an end, no fulfillment capable of satisfying man's desires. The circular concept of history (of time) is radically pessimistic. Man is locked into the circle of time, on the treadmill of history. Here there is no exit.

Within this religious concept, man can discover a way out only through a cultic identification with a God achieved through a liturgical mystery that is a representation of a mythical adventure of this God—for example, a death and a resurrection. The mythical idea of death and resurrection is suggested by the sequence of the seasons, and particularly by the natural cycle of vegetative life.

The salvation offered by such religions is individual. The individuals can be saved by way of the liturgical mystery. But history, the collective human adventure, cannot be redeemed. It has to be accepted as it is, and to be escaped from by means of the cultic religion into an absolutely metahistorical salvation.

The ethicoprophetic type of religion corresponds to the biblical religion of ancient Israel and to the religion of Jesus and of the first Christians, as presented or reflected in the New Testament.

This religion has an open linear concept (we might say straight-line concept) of historic time.

God is the liberator, and the liberation that God promises and the believer hopes for is historic. The purpose proposed is to make real in historic mankind the freeing of the oppressed, to establish the kingdom of justice, the fullness of brotherhood and of love.

From this it follows that the essential quality of this type of religion is ethicoprophetic. Religion calls on man to make justice and love real. The place reserved for cult in mystery religions is here allotted to the love that works justice. This comes out very clearly in a text from the New Testament in which the prophetic thrust of ancient Israel can be deeply felt: "Pure, unspoiled religion, in the eyes of God our Father is this: coming to the help of orphans and widows when they need it, and keeping oneself uncontaminated by the world" (Jm. 1:27). This phrase is enormously expressive, because the word "religion," which in the original Greek is *threskeía*, is the word employed technically to identify cultic religiosity, and sometimes, even, an obsession with cult. It is clear, in consequence, that the text of St. James rejects ontological-cultist religion and insists emphatically on an ethico-prophetic approach to religion.

Since my present purpose is not to give an exhaustive study but only to explain my faith as clearly as lies in my power, I shall not delay further with this point.

The prophets of Israel condemn an obsessive concern with cult. More than that, one might say that they waver between a total rejection of sacrificial liturgical cult and a condemnation of obsessive concern with cult, without rejecting that cult whose meaning is properly understood and that protects the absolute priority over the cultic activities of the obligation to work justice in a spirit of faith.

The religious concept of the New Testament becomes more complex because it incorporates the "mystery" of Christ, who died and rose from the dead, and of an identification of the believer with Christ, an identification that St. Paul tells us becomes effective in a special and privileged way in the sacramental symbolism of baptism.

There is no doubt that this concept contains a dangerous analogy with the ontological-cultist attitude of the mystery religions that formed the environment of St. Paul's world.

This analogy has unfortunately produced very harmful effects throughout the history of Christianity, with the result that the religion of Christians (and specifically of Catholics) is today preponderantly an ontological-cultic religion. In addition, the activity of the ecclesiastical "apparatus" is directed fundamentally to the preservation of an ontological-cultist religion against the incipient movements springing up spontaneously in the Church that seek to recover ethicoprophetic religious attitudes in their fullness.

I am well aware that the analogy between the cultic "mystery" religions and the New Testament concept of the "mystery" of Christ dying and rising again can cause some (or many) Christians to give up their Christian faith. It is, I believe, true that there exists a qualitative difference between the myths of the "mystery" religions and the dogmas explained to us by St. Paul and in the Johannine writings. In addition, the Christian concept found in the New Testament has a certain articulation with historic facts that puts it on a plane different from that on which the "myths" of the Greco-Oriental "mystery" religions move. But in any case, we are here facing an unsolved problem that confirms once again the radical experience that faith rests freely on the grace of an interior revelation, and that the help science can give to the motives for believing is always inadequate.

I believe in the resurrection of Christ. The resurrection is for me, in "faith," a "mysterious event," and in consequence it is not in the proper sense a "myth." But it is not an event that can be demonstrated historically. It is not even an "historic" event, because it does not and cannot pertain to the web of empirical and phenomenological realities that constitute "history" and that are the object of the science of (positive) history. But to say it is not an "historical event" is not to say that it is not a "mysteriously real" event, to which man can attain only in "the mystery of faith."

The principal difficulty for believing in the "mystery" of Christ is not to be found, however, in my opinion, in the "dangerous analogy" that may exist between the concept of Paul or of John and the viewpoint of the Greek-Asian "mystery" religions. The real difficulty results from the fact that Christians (and concretely, Catholics) have not known how to escape the danger and have fallen into an ontological-cultist concept of Christianity. The analogy in this way becomes much more substantial, and the scandal for the faith that results can be overcome only by making oneself vigorously aware that the Christianity lived by Christians (unlike that of Paul or of the Gospels) is an ontological-cultist religion, and as such a false religion, justly denounced by Marx as something it is necessary to rise above.

Only by reconversion of the religion of Christians to the plane of ethicoprophetic religion can we ensure a solid credibility for Christianity.

The "mystery" of Christ dead and risen from the dead, as a "mystery" of an ethicoprophetic religion of love and justice, and as a "mystery of faith" articulated in a messianic historical and eschatological hope, is essentially different from the pagan "mysteries" of the Greco-Oriental religious movements of the Hellenic world. On the other hand, Christianity in its present form, narrowed almost completely to the dimensions of an ontological-cultist religious expression, is not very different as a type of religious attitude from the paganism of the "mysteries."

But that was not the case with the Christianity of the New Testament writers.

And above all, that was not the case with the religion expressed by Jesus.

At the level of history, I see no reason to entertain serious doubts about the following statements. Jesus was a prophet, situated in the line of the prophets of Israel, in the sense of his uncompromising denunciation of the injustice of the powerful. Jesus anathematized the accumulation of riches, the fruit and the basis of the selfishness of the "rich," and an element in the unjust oppression of the dispossessed. Jesus carried to the extreme limit his fellowship and identification with the humble, the oppressed, and the poor. For all of this, Jesus was condemned to death by a Roman court as a political agitator. An important element in bringing this to pass was the conflict between Jesus and a priestly caste concerned about its own privileges, immersed in politics, and opposed to prophets. By contrast, the line of eschatological hope stands out vividly in Jesus, a fact that also removes him absolutely from the ontological-cultic type of religion.

When Paul speaks of the mysterious incorporation of Christians in Christ, of a mysterious identification of the Christian with the glorified body of Christ, the "dynamism" of this mystery is not contained in an ontological-cultist type of religion but in an ethicoprophetic type. The reason is the role that "faith that makes its power felt through love" (Ga. 5:6) plays for Paul, the Pauline dialectic of love and justice, and the explicit interrelationship of faith in the resurrection with eschatological hope.

It follows from this that the insertion of the "mystery" of Christ, "who was put to death for our sins and raised to life to justify us" (Rm. 4:25), does not represent in Paul a lapse into an ontological-cultist concept of religion.

Neither are we turned in the direction of an ontological-cultist religion by the mysticism of the Johannine writings. They are absolutely firmly rooted in the realism of brotherly love, the one thing that is both indispensable and sufficient to make us children of truth and children of God.

> We have passed out of death and into life,
> and of this we can be sure
> because we love our brothers.
> If you refuse to love, you must remain dead;
> to hate your brother is to be a murderer,
> and murderers, as you know, do not have eternal life in them.

This has taught us love—
that he gave up his life for us;
and we, too, ought to give up our lives for our brothers.
If a man who was rich enough in this world's goods
saw that one of his brothers was in need,
but closed his heart to him,
how could the love of God be living in him?
My children,
Our love is not to be just words or mere talk,
but something real and active;
only by this can we be certain
that we are children of the truth
and be able to quiet our conscience in his presence,
whatever accusations it may raise against us,
because God is greater than our conscience and he knows
    everything.

(I Jn. 3:14–20)

My present situation within the Christian community is para-doxical. My faith in Christ Jesus keeps me in this community. But my understanding of faith in Jesus Christ makes me feel a stranger in that community, which taken as a whole and to the extent that it is represented by the ecclesiastical establishment, maintains a religious attitude that is predominantly (if not ex-clusively) ontological-cultist.

The solution of this conflict for me is not to reduce the Christian community to the tiny group of those I meet who think as I do, and to try to form with these a new "church." This was, more or less, the approach of the sixteenth-century reformers. The great reformers had much more than a small group with them. In any case, neither the historic and psychosociological experience of the reform movements, nor my own reflection on the faith, nor the impulse of the Spirit (which I hope I may not wholly lack) drive me to break with the community of those who believe in Christ to establish another community of believers. It is important to understand, after all the discussion, that the faith of these and of those (imperfect to whatever degree it may be, no matter how bastardized) does not end—to the extent that it still is "faith" —in our teaching and understanding of the faith, but in Jesus who died and rose from the dead, and who is above us all and above all our "understandings."

Neither do I regard it as a solution to deny the historic community of Christians so that I can take refuge in a kind of Platonic idea of the Church. The ethicoprophetic, messianic, and eschatological religious attitude that is found in the Bible does not allow us to flee historic reality in this way.

I am a Christian because I believe in Jesus Christ. I am historically within the community of the believers (a real, historic believer), and concretely in the Catholic Church.

Within this community I cannot do other than profess my faith. It is a faith that finds itself in conflict with the way the majority of my brothers in the faith see and live their Christian life.

It is a faith which, within the real lowliness I recognize as mine, seeks to help others to live the faith and to find the ethicoprophetic vein of true Christianity.

I cannot do other.

I thus live at my modest level that experience of St. Paul, who continued on his course to see if he might thus succeed in taking hold of Christ Jesus, because of one fundamental fact: Christ Jesus had "seized hold" of him.

5. The Second Commandment of the Decalogue and the Work of the Prophets

IF STUDY OF KARL MARX helped me to become aware of the falsity of a Christianity of an ontological-cultist type, the reading of the prophets of the Bible enlightened me farther along this road.

The entire message of the prophets can be said to come down

to two issues: the denunciation and absolute rejection of worship that is joined to social injustice, and the equally energetic denunciation and rejection of religious syncretism joining the worship of Yahweh to that of the Baals, the pagan gods of their neighbors.

The rejection of worship that is allied to injustice is expressed in words that carry an overwhelming intensity of feeling. This is already apparent in Amos, the oldest of the prophets whose communications are conserved in the Bible.

> I hate and despise your feasts,
> I take no pleasure in your solemn festivals.
> When you offer me holocausts, . . .
> I reject your oblations,
> and refuse to look at your sacrifices of fattened cattle.
> Let me have no more of the din of your chanting,
> no more of your strumming on harps.
> But let justice flow like water,
> and integrity like an unfailing stream.
>
> (Amos 5:21–24)

The espousal of the people to Yahweh (the Covenant) could take place for Hosea only "with integrity and justice, with tenderness and love" (Ho. 2:21).

Micah explains where the true religious attitude, pleasing to Yahweh, is to be found. Its home is not in a cultic religion but in one that is ethicoprophetic. The text of the prophet speaks for itself.

> With what gift shall I come into Yahweh's presence
> and bow down before God on high?
> Shall I come with holocausts,
> with calves one year old?
> Will he be pleased with rams by the thousand,
> with libations of oil in torrents?
> Must I give my first-born for what I have done wrong,
> the fruit of my body for my own sin?

—What is good has been explained to you, man;
this is what Yahweh asks of you:
only this, to act justly,
to love tenderly
and to walk humbly with your God.

(Mi. 6:6–8)

The establishment of justice in history appears in Isaiah as the
work of Yahweh, the Lord, and as the content of messianic hope.

The people that walked in darkness
has seen a great light;
on those who live in a land of deep shadow
a light has shone.
You have made their gladness greater,
you have made their joy increase;
they rejoice in your presence
as men rejoice at harvest time,
as men are happy when they are dividing the spoils.
For the yoke that was weighing on him,
the bar across his shoulders,
the rod of his oppressor,
these you break as on the day of Midian.
For all the footgear of battle,
every cloak rolled in blood,
is burned,
and consumed by fire.
For there is a child born for us,
a son given to us
and dominion is laid on his shoulders;
and this is the name they give him:
Wonder Counselor, Mighty God,
Eternal Father, Prince of Peace.
Wide is his dominion
in a peace that has no end,
for the throne of David

and for his royal power,
which he establishes and makes secure
in justice and integrity.
From this time onward and for ever,
the jealous love of Yahweh Sabaoth will do this.

(Is. 9:1–6)

There is an extraordinarily expressive passage in the book of
Jeremiah. The ontological-cultist religion, with its lack of concern
for social and historic justice—which inevitably converts it into
an instrument of injustice and a cloak for oppression—is false,
even when it pretends to be directed to the true God, to Yahweh,
the Lord. This passage retains the same pertinence for today's
Catholics that it had for the inhabitants of Judah in the sixth
century before Christ.

The word that was addressed to Jeremiah by Yahweh,
"Go and stand at the gate of the Temple of Yahweh
and there proclaim this message.
Say, 'Listen to the word of Yahweh,
all you men of Judah
who come in by these gates to worship Yahweh.
Yahweh Sabaoth, the God of Israel says this:
Amend your behavior and your actions
and I will stay with you here in this place.
Put no trust in delusive words like these:
This is the sanctuary of Yahweh,
the sanctuary of Yahweh, the sanctuary of Yahweh!
But if you do amend your behavior and your actions,
if you treat each other fairly,
if you do not exploit the stranger, the orphan and the widow
(if you do not shed innocent blood in this place),
and if you do not follow alien gods, to your own ruin,
then here in this place I will stay with you,
in the land that long ago I gave to your fathers for ever.

65

Yet here you are,
trusting in delusive words, to no purpose!
Steal, would you, murder, commit adultery, perjure your-
    selves,
burn incense to Baal,
follow alien gods that you do not know?
—and then come presenting yourselves
in this Temple that bears my name,
saying: Now we are safe—
safe to go on committing all these abominations!
Do you take this Temple that bears my name
for a robbers' den?
I, at any rate, am not blind—
it is Yahweh who speaks. . . .' "

(Jr. 7:1–11)

In my journey of "mental conversion," with the prophets
lighting the way for me, I was helped to take a further step forward by an extraordinary book written by my friend, José Porfirio
Miranda. Its title is *Marx and the Bible: A Critique of the
Philosophy of Oppression*, and it was published in Mexico in
1971.

Not all the analyses made by Miranda convince me 100 percent.
His interpretation of the Letter to the Romans seems to me to
contain an extrapolation and a one-sided perspective. But the
basic intuitions are impressive and very exact. His biblical analysis
of the Old Testament provided new light for me. Its basic thrust
could be rejected only by minds that had been unconsciously
conditioned by a false ontological-cultist attitude.

Miranda has made me appreciate the importance of the second
commandment of the biblical Decalogue. And this understanding
is of extreme value in order to recognize the tragedy of the
"paganism" of Christians.

The focal point, from which one must look at the content of the
Pentateuch in order to understand its inner meaning, is the

66

appearance of God to Moses as described in Exodus. Here precisely is the "revelation" of the God of Israel.

All that went before is by way of a prologue to this moment, which is truly "the beginning."

And Yahweh said, "I have seen the miserable state of my people in Egypt. I have heard their appeal to be free of their slave drivers. Yes, I am well aware of their sufferings. I mean to deliver them. . . ." (Ex. 3:7–8). "And now the cry of the sons of Israel has come to me, and I have witnessed the way in which the Egyptians oppress them." (Ex. 3:9). Then Moses said to God, "I am to go then, to the sons of Israel and say to them, 'The God of your fathers has sent me to you.' But if they ask me what his name is, what am I to tell them?" And God said to Moses, "I Am who I Am. This," he added, "is what you must say to the sons of Israel: 'I Am has sent me to you.'" (Ex. 3:13–14).

Today we know reasonably well the meaning of this mysterious dialogue. In the Semitic culture, to know the name of a thing was the equivalent of possessing the essential knowledge that ensured a certain power over that thing. Genesis tells us that Yahweh brought all the animals of the field and all the birds of the air before the man "to see what he would call them" and so that each one would "bear the name the man would give it" (Gn. 2:19). It is within this cultural context that the meaning of God's reply emerges. "I Am who I Am" does not mean that God is providing a concept or construct of his being, an ontological description of himself. Quite the contrary. God refuses to express his essence. The best translation for us of "I Am who I Am" would be: "I am I." And that is enough. You cannot know my inner essence. But you should know that I am here, and that I want the liberation of my oppressed people, and that you can (and must) count on me.

It is entirely proper and necessary to seek to explore more fully the meaning of this revelation of Yahweh, the "I Am," the only God of Israel.

The refusal to give his name signified his absolute transcendence. He is the "invisible" God. But the denial is presented in this form: I do not tell you my name, but I do tell you that I am here, that I offer myself, because I have heard the cries of the oppressed and I have seen the oppression. And I am against oppression and on the side of the oppressed.

What this means is that God gives us no "ontological" revelation about his essence, other than to reveal his absolute transcendence, which leaves him in the realm of mystery: I Am I; don't ask me anything further. But he does reveal to us his judgment on history. He reveals to us what might be called his ethical essence, his action as Lord and Judge of history and of life. This is the same God who challenges Cain, his brother's assassin.

Yahweh asked Cain, "Where is your brother Abel?" "I do not know," he replied. "Am I my brother's guardian?" "What have you done?" Yahweh asked. "Listen to the sound of your brother's blood, crying out to me from the ground." (Gn. 4:9–10).

The deep meaning of this really extraordinary and unique aspect of the biblical revelation of God is the following: We can truly reach God only by making conscience the intermediary. He is an invisible God, but he does intervene, and he intervenes on behalf of the oppressed, against oppression, on the side of justice, of mercy, and of love. He is the God of the prophets. In consequence, an ontological-cultist religion, which is not primarily (and, in a certain way, exclusively) ethicoprophetical, is not the true religion.

In this context one can grasp all the force of the second commandment of the biblical Decalogue. To understand it better, let us look at it together with the first commandment:

I am Yahweh your God who brought you out of the land of Egypt, out of the house of slavery.
You shall have no gods except me.
You shall not make yourselves a carved image or any likeness of anything in heaven or on earth beneath or in the waters under

the earth; you shall not bow down to them nor serve them. For I, Yahweh your God, am a jealous God and I punish the father's fault in the sons, the grandsons, and the great-grandsons of those who hate me; but I show kindness to thousands of those who love me and keep my commandments.

(Ex. 20:2–6; Dt. 5:6–10)

What this second commandment forbids is not idolatry in the form of worship of gods other than Yahweh. That kind of idolatry is forbidden by the first commandment. What the second commandment forbids is "to make for oneself an image of God" in order to worship it.

This prohibition can be understood in its superficial meaning or in a deeper meaning.

On the level of superficial meaning, its content is clear.

At the deeper level, it is also clear but not so easy to explain.

To make for oneself an image of God is to "ontologize" God, so that we can relate to him without finding ourselves *before everything else* in the presence of the ethicoprophetic God who will challenge us about our brothers, just as Yahweh challenged Cain, Moses, and the Egyptian Pharaoh.

To ontologize God is to convert the invisible God, who speaks and challenges our conscience on the issues of justice and brotherhood, into a visible God who "is" before he "speaks" and whom I know as an "essence" and not simply and in the first instance through his prophetic voice.

With this kind of God I can establish a relationship *before* he can ask me about my brothers or can demand from me the freeing of the oppressed.

And this relationship with such a God, occurring before any challenge from him to me concerning my brothers, becomes the primary and most important element. Such a relationship is expressed in a form of "worship" which, for as long as it is understood and established in this way, is not identified with a commitment on the side of justice and liberation. The reason is that the issue of my brothers is now, inescapably, a secondary problem.

69

In the ontological-cultist type of religion, what is truly important is faith as the acceptance of some doctrinal formulas, and a worship of the "being" of God. This God can in due course establish moral regulations concerning relations with other men. But the inescapably adjectival character that such demands take on makes them necessarily ambiguous and inoperative.

In addition, a cultist religion becomes inevitably entangled in the establishment of a priestly "cast," which holds "power" over "the sphere of religion," and to which it pertains sociologically (and juridically) to make this power effective for the faithful of that religion. In short, the concrete structure of the "apparatus" of the cultist religious community makes it impossible to orient the ethical duties that the religion may impose primarily and effectively in the direction of justice and the freeing of the oppressed. The reason is that an "apparatus" of power (of privilege) cannot, historically and socially, be radically oriented toward confrontation with other powers, but rather toward compromise with them.

In all these ways and by all these devices, the ontological-cultist type of religious organization is really an instrument of injustice and oppression, an obstacle to the historic liberation of man, the "opium of the people." Marx's analysis is absolutely precise.

The second commandment of the biblical Decalogue, by condemning an ontological-cultist kind of religion, sets us on the path of an ethicoprophetic religion that is not an "opium of the people." But unfortunately, this commandment in its deeper sense has been unknown in the greatest measure both to the ancient Israelites and to Christians.

Unfortunately our Catholic Church understood this second commandment only in its superficial and strictly literal sense. And since it did not feel itself obliged to avoid anthropomorphic representations of the Father in religious art, it decided simply to suppress this second commandment of the Decalogue. After this amputation, the tenth commandment of the biblical Decalogue was split in two in order to maintain the number of ten.

The tenth commandment of the biblical Decalogue says: "You shall not covet your neighbor's house. You shall not covet your neighbor's wife, or his servant, man or woman, or his ox, or his donkey, or anything that is his." (Ex. 20:17). Our catechisms have separated as the ninth commandment the prohibition against coveting one's neighbor's wife, leaving as tenth commandment the prohibition against coveting the goods of another.

The cultural fact of this slight manipulation of the Decalogue would not be important, were it not that the suppression of the second commandment followed from a lack of understanding of its deeper meaning. This lack of understanding has had the result that the type of religion conducted by our Catholic Church has been, on the whole, ontological-cultist.

And nevertheless, the New Testament is as radically oriented toward ethicoprophetic religion as is the Mosaic revelation of Exodus. Here, for example, is what St. John's first Letter says:

We can be sure that we know God
only by keeping his commandments.
Anyone who says, "I know him,"
and does not keep his commandments,
is a liar,
refusing to admit the truth.

(I Jn. 2:3–4)

Anyone who claims to be in the light
but hates his brother
is still in the dark.
But anyone who loves his brother is living in the light
and need not be afraid of stumbling.

(I Jn. 2:9–10)

In this way we distinguish the children of God
from the children of the devil:

71

anybody not living a holy life
and not loving his brother
is no child of God's.

(I Jn. 3:10)

My dear people,
let us love one another
since love comes from God
and everyone who loves is begotten by God and knows God.
Anyone who fails to love can never have known God,
because God is love.

(I Jn. 4:7–8)

No one has ever seen God;
but as long as we love one another
God will live in us
and his love will be complete in us.

(I Jn. 4:12)

Anyone who says, "I love God,"
and hates his brother,
is a liar,
since a man who does not love the brother that he can see
cannot love God, whom he has never seen.

(I Jn. 4:20)

Having reached this point, I cannot avoid a question:

If the true religion is ethicoprophetic, whereas the religion that
—taken as a whole—the Catholic Church conducts is ontological-
cultist, how can I in good conscience stay in the Catholic Church?

I shall offer some further thoughts on this point later.

For the present, I think it enough to say that, according to my
conscience, remaining in the Church is to be conditioned by
two factors: first, that one should not reject ethicoprophetic
religion and should denounce the deviation from the right course
that ontological-cultist religion represents, exerting all his energies
to eliminate it in himself and in others; second, that one keeps

clearly in mind that the Catholic Church, and all churches that claim to be Christian and regard faith in Christ as their starting point, are called to convert themselves to the ethicoprophetic religion of the crucified and glorified Jesus, who is to come to give its final fulfillment to history. And if there is a calling, there is hope of conversion. What the price will be, God will decide.

As regards Baptism and the Eucharist, it seems to me sufficiently clear that these are conceived in the New Testament in a spirit of confession, of supplication, of hope, and of "commitment" to justice and brotherly love. On the other hand, within the historic reality of the Church they are usually conceived as performing an ontological-cultist function.

The Eucharist is for me something very important and precious. But I try to live it as a mediating action of an ethicoprophetic form of religion. Between the Supper of the Lord, which is commemorated with a living remembrance of faith, and the *Parousia* (return of the Lord), for which we hope, every Eucharist is a repetition of the prophetic cry: "Come, Lord Jesus" (Rv. 22:20).

6. Christianity of Love and of Justice

WHILE LECTURING in Barcelona in 1970 and 1971, it occurred to me to suggest the layout of that city as a symbol of the way I envisage true Christianity. There is a great central plaza, up from which leads a broad boulevard. Avenues with pedestrian walks in the center of the roadway go down in the opposite direction, and to the right there is a transverse road.

The great central plaza of Christianity is love of one's neighbor.

The boulevard that rises is faith-love-hope in Christ, and through and in Christ, in God.

The footpaths running down the avenues represent the real drive of justice, the commitment to justice, against repression, the effort to achieve the historic liberation of man.

73

The transverse road is the life of worship. But I described this transverse road as a one-way street, *toward* (not *away from*) the central square. Worship, in the understanding of a Christianity that is genuine, is for love and justice, and not the other way around.

Worship either is an expression of lived love and justice (since these are the qualities that in ethicoprophetic religion occupy the position allotted to the "sacred" cult in cultist religion), or it is a prayer to God beseeching from him the "grace" that will convert our heart to love and justice.

Some may object that this layout of the "city of God" is not correct, because the central place is that of faith in God and love of him. I reply that that is the ontological-cultist concept. In the ethicoprophetic concept, love of one's neighbor is, so to speak, the sacrament of the love of God. And this quasisacramental road is the only one. It is not possible to love the invisible God unless one loves visible man, with the tangible works of love.

Christ is to be found in the oppressed whom we are working to set free, and nowhere else. That is the inner meaning of the parable of the final judgment recounted in St. Matthew's Gospel (Mt. 25:31–46).

For some years I have seen in verses 14 and 15 of Chapter 4 of St. Paul's Letter to the Ephesians one of the most precise expressions of the ethicoprophetic character of authentic Christianity. The "truth" of our faith becomes "real" in genuine love of our neighbor, and this genuine love inescapably introduces the problem of justice and liberation. This is where the truth of the Christian religion is "verified." But this verification, which gives a positive result as far as the true religion of Jesus is concerned, gives a result that is far more negative than positive when applied to the religion of Christians.

In a book, *Christian Attitudes to Social Problems*, published in Barcelona in 1967, I offered the following analysis of Ephesians 4:14–15:

The original Greek text is of a richness that is untranslatable, and that calls for an extended explanation.

In the context (Ep. 4:11–13), St. Paul states that Christ has distributed his gifts to the saints for the work of the ministry, which is directed to the building up of the body of Christ, a task the completion of which will bring us to form all together a single entity in faith and in our knowledge of the Son of God, and to become the perfect man, fully mature with the fullness of Christ himself.

The thought here expressed by Paul is extremely condensed. The Church is the body of Christ.[7] This body is living, but it is still in the process of growth, still being developed. The gifts of Christ are the instruments of this living growth (what today we would call the hormones essential to growth). The dynamic orientation of the living growth of the Church is a fullness of faith, which is vitally unifying, and which will bring the body to maturity of age and strength. This body will then have acquired dimensions proportioned to its head, namely, Christ. And then the vital inflowing of Christ will possess his body in its entirety. Christ will be in this body, which will be perfectly incorporated into him, a "fullness" that will be realized in the total communion of the body with its head, Christ.

After this dazzling synthesis, Paul moves on to describe in verse 14 what the fullness of faith *is not*, and in verse 15 what this "life" in faith, which constitutes the perfect maturity of the Christian community, *is*.

According to verse 14, the faith that realizes the fullness of Christ in us is the overcoming (denial) of an infantile faith (in the disparaging sense of the word infantile), which leaves us at the mercy of every wind of doctrine, the plaything of the deceptions of men and of their cunning ways of leading us astray into error.

But what, positively, is this "full life" of faith that incorporates Christians perfectly into Christ, making of them in Christ the perfect man who realizes the "fullness" of Christ?

7 In a later work I drew attention to the fact that when Paul says that "the Church is the body of Christ," he does not mean a "social body" belonging to Christ, but the living, mysterious body of the risen Christ. The Christians, as "people" of God, are incorporated, assimilated mysteriously into the body of Christ. On this point I was enlightened by reading John A. T. Robinson, *Body: A Study in Pauline Theology* (Chicago: Regnery, 1952); also by P. Benoit's "Corps, tête et plérome dans les épîtres de la captivité," *Revue biblique* 63 (1956), pp. 5–44.

St. Paul presents the answer to this question in verse 15. The life of faith consists of this, that "if we live by the truth and in love, we shall grow in all ways into Christ, who is the head." This is the Vulgate text. . . . But the original Greek (untranslatable) has further overtones. The phrase "to live by the truth" corresponds to a single Greek word, *aletheúontes*, for which there is no equivalent verb in Latin or in our modern languages. This word (a verb derived from the substantive *alétheia*, meaning "truth") would be translated literally by a verb meaning "to be the living truth" ("lived"). An exact translation, according to the sense, of this verse 15 of Chapter 4 of the Letter to the Ephesians, would be: "Being in our own very existence the lived and living truth by the power of love, we shall grow in every way toward (within) the One who is the head, Christ."

What is most important in this text is the role love plays, and its relation to faith. Love is the essential *mediation*. Through it, faith is "lived" and human existence is converted into "living" and "lived truth," that is to say, into "authentic" faith, "true" faith.

It is perfectly clear that for St. Paul, "faith" and "love" are not two separate things added to each other, but rather that the two, in a vital association, form one "life," which is "lived truth."

Without the *mediation* (the molding energy) of love, faith is not faith in the full and authentic sense. It is not "true" faith in the "living" sense. Even if a Christian should pronounce all the articles of faith, and be ready to die—and perhaps to kill—for each and every one of them, if he has not charity, his faith is not "true" in the innermost meaning in which St. Paul here speaks. The reason is that the faith this Christian professes is not "living truth" but only the abstract affirmation of another's truth, which is not the object of testimony as a "living" truth in the believer.

St. Paul teaches here that there is no "true" faith, with "living truth" except *in* (through, by force of) love. But love, for St. Paul as for St. John, is love of one's neighbor in which love of God is expressed. In the famous hymn to love of Chapter 13 of the first Letter to the Corinthians, St. Paul describes love, which is greater than faith or hope (I Co. 13:13), and which "does not come to an end" (I Co. 13:8), in terms of brotherly love for other people (I Co. 13:4–7). The reason is a profound one. In the Letter to Titus (3:4), St. Paul uses the Greek word "philanthropia" when he presents Jesus Christ as the revelation of the *philanthropy* (the love for mankind) of God. This means that the love of God is inseparable from the love of men. There is no love of God without loving our fellow men. Christ is the revelation and the sacrament of the "philanthropy" of God, and anyone who shuts himself off from "philanthropy" shuts himself off from the revelation of God.

St. John also says, in his First Letter (4:7–8), that "anyone who fails to love (his neighbor) can never have known God, because God is love" (because of the context, this can only be the saving love of God for mankind, the "philanthropy" of which St. Paul spoke). Our faith, St. John adds (I Jn. 4:16) consists of having "known and put our faith in God's love toward ourselves." It follows that, as St. John also insists most emphatically, "anyone who says, 'I love God,' and hates his brother, is a liar, since a man who does not love the brother that he can see cannot love God, whom he has never seen." (I Jn. 4:20).

We have thus established for us in St. Paul and in St. John an essential unity of "life," faith, and love, a love that is directed to our neighbor as *mediation* and essential manifestation of the love of God.

This all-embracing and living idea of faith, as the life of faith under the impulse of love, which is the love of communion of God and of our neighbor, was excellently expressed by St. Augustine in his commentary on the Gospel of St. John. St. Augustine distinguishes between "believing Jesus" and "believing on Jesus." The former would mean an intellectual acceptance of the word of Jesus. The latter is a living self-surrender to the word of Jesus. This kind of faith is "faith-affection-love-communion with one's neighbor." Or, as St. Augustine puts it: "What then is 'to believe on him'? By believing to love him, by believing to esteem highly, by believing to go into him and to be incorporated in his members."[8]

Now St. Paul takes us to a new and still deeper level, namely, that of the essential dynamic unity of love and justice. It is a central theme of the Letter to the Romans.

The Letter of St. Paul to the Romans begins by establishing that neither the gentiles nor the Jews had been able to fulfill the obligations of justice (Rm. 1:18–3:20). It is God who justifies by

[8] *Quid est ergo credere in eum? Credendo amare, credendo diligere, credendo in eum ire et eius membris incorporari.* St. Augustine, *In Ioan. Evang.* tr. 29, n. 6; Pl. 35, 1631. English trans., Philip Schaff, ed. *Nicene and Post-Nicene Fathers* (Grand Rapids, Mich.: B. Eerdmans, 1956), VII, 185.

means of faith in Jesus Christ, by a free gift in virtue of the redemption accomplished in Jesus Christ (Rm. 3:22–24). But the life of the Christian justified in Christ Jesus is the life of the spirit, because the Holy Spirit gives himself to us, as a pledge of the love of God, which is poured out on us (Rm. 5:5), to be the driving force of our life of love—love of our neighbor and of God in Christ (Rm. 8:9 and 14–15; Ga. 5:1 and 13). This being so, the love of the neighbor, which flows from the impulse of the Holy Spirit dwelling in the believer, and which is life in the spirit and in freedom, must necessarily—by virtue of its innermost dynamism—perform all the demands of justice. Such is the argument of Chapter 13 of the Letter to the Romans: "Pay every government official what he has a right to ask—whether it be direct tax or indirect, fear or honor. Avoid getting into debt, except the debt of mutual love. If you love your fellow men you have carried out your obligations. All the commandments: You shall not commit adultery, you shall not kill, you shall not steal, you shall not covet, and so on, are summed up in this single command: You must love your neighbor as yourself. Love is the one thing that cannot hurt your neighbor; that is why it is the answer to every one of the commandments." (13:7–10).

The teaching of St. Paul in the Letter to the Ephesians, the First Letter to the Corinthians, and the Letters to Titus, to the Galatians, and to the Romans, have in this way brought out for us the "meaning" of Christian "existence": a faith through which man is spiritually liberated to live in Christ love of his neighbor in communion with God, working justice with all his strength in his dealings with others, this being the living reality of the "truth" of his faith. And that is what the author of the Pauline Letter to the Hebrews calls "grace," urging them in return "to worship God in the way he finds acceptable, in reverence and fear" (Heb. 12:28). It is also what St. Peter in his first Letter calls "spiritual sacrifices," which constitute the cultic action of that "holy priesthood" that is the "life" of Christians incorporated into Christ (I P. 2:4–5).

It follows, accordingly, that liturgical worship in the strict sense and sacramental life are meaningless except as a *means* to enable the Christian to reach, through the liturgy and the sacraments, that other living liturgy of the "priesthood" of all Christians, which is the "living truth" of the faith by virtue of love, of a love that works justice in all its fullness. We can say that the *content* of the liturgical sacraments, the *res* (thing) of the sacrament in the language of the medieval theologians, is this dynamic of faith-love-justice that is the "truth" of Christian "existence" as "lived faith." Without this content, sacramental life lacks all meaning.

This commanding view of Christianity offered us by the New Testament raises a question for the believer that he must face. Why is the Christianity of Christians in the course of history so different from the Christian plan formulated in the New Testament and lived, at least to some extent, by the Christians of the apostolic age?

How can the believer in Christ resolve for himself the shocking fact of Christianity's failure in history?

The first thing the believer must do is not to close his eyes to the disturbing fact.

It is, of course, evident that the Church (or churches) guarded the books of the New Testament throughout the course of history. They did not allow them to fall from their hands in a material or literal sense.

In the New Testament they brought along a grain of mustard seed, a piece of leaven, and that could not fail to have some impact.

The Christian communities have in consequence, throughout history, been a cultivated field (or a mass of dough) of evangelical and Christian fermentations. But the Christian mass as a whole has not fermented. The ecclesial field has not been covered with the ripening grain from the evangelical seed. Rather, the seed and the small piece of leaven have remained buried in an "ecclesiastical" (clerical) historic and social reality centered not on the liberating love that works justice, but on worship and clerical power, on a safe, middle-of-the-road course in politics, and on an attitude of social reformism that does not go beyond the verbal level.

How then can the believer who begins to discover the reality of the biblical and evangelical demands face up to the problem that the Church concretely creates for his Christian faith?

I shall offer some reflections on this question, which is necessarily complex for the believer in Christ, shortly.

First, however, I want to deal with the following question.

Where exactly is the waterway in which Christianity as lived in the Christian community (of the churches, and specifically of the Catholic Church) foundered in the course of history?

During a visit to Germany in 1958, I had occasion to read the book written by Antanas Maceina on the mystery of evil, an effort to construct a theology of the history of the Adversary of Christ as an explanation of the account of Antichrist given by Vladimir Sergeyevich Soloviev, nineteenth-century Russian religious philosopher and poet.[9]

In this closely reasoned book, I came for the first time across an allegorical explanation of the Gospel passage of the three temptations of Christ in the desert. The Gospels (Matthew and Luke) present Christ to us as tempted and overcoming temptation. In actual fact, it is the Church that has been tempted. And the Church, unlike Christ, has succumbed to the temptation, if not at all times and in all its members, at least in the general course of its historic development up to the present time.

For the Church, the temptation of the food ("Tell these stones to turn into loaves," Mt. 4:3) is the temptation of wealth. The temptation of the miracle ("Throw yourself down; for Scripture says: He will put you in his angels' charge, and they will support you in their hands," Mt. 4:6) is the temptation of exclusive reliance on the sacramental powers to the neglect of personal holiness. (As I put it, this is the abandonment of an ethico-prophetic attitude to religion in favor of the ontological-cultist approach.) The temptation of power ("I will give you all these—all the kingdoms of the world and their splendor—if you fall at my feet and worship me," Mt. 4:9) is the tendency to carry the work of redemption forward by political means and not by apos-

[9] *Das Geheimnis der Bosheit.* Versucht einer Geschichtstheologie des Widersachers Christi als Deutung der Erzahlung vom AntiChrist Solowjews. Freiburg (Baden), 1955.

tolic testimony. This tendency toward a pastoral of "domination," organically integrated into the political, cultural, and social power (or to quasipolitical power inside the ecclesial community itself), enmeshes the Church by its intrinsic logic in the dialectic of master and slave, forcing it inescapably to identify (in more or less complex and disguised ways) with the historic forces that represent the "master."

The three temptations of food, miracle, and power combine organically into complex relationships and mutual influences. But according to the first Letter of St. Paul to Timothy, the most fundamental of them is the temptation of food. This letter speaks of religious teachers "who are neither rational nor informed and imagine that religion is a way of making a profit" (I Tm. 6:5). St. Paul's attitude is very different: "Religion, of course, does bring large profits, but only to those who are content with what they have. We brought nothing into the world, and we can take nothing out of it; but as long as we have food and clothing, let us be content with that. People who long to be rich are a prey to temptation; they get trapped into all sorts of foolish and dangerous ambitions which eventually plunge them into ruin and destruction. 'The love of money (*philargyría*) is the root of all evils' and there are some who, pursuing it, have wandered away from the faith, and so given their souls any number of fatal wounds." (I Tm. 6:6–10).

7. Christianity and Money

DURING THE 1936–37 ACADEMIC YEAR I was studying ethics, which was the subject for the third year of my philosophy course, in an ecclesiastical college that the Spanish Jesuits had opened in Belgium in 1933. The principle that insisted that private property, including ownership of the means of production, was established by the "natural law," was then considered to be obligatory for

Catholics, as a result of its repeated affirmation in papal encyclicals.

Even at that time, nevertheless, taking into account the situation that then prevailed and the limited nature of the opportunity for critical reflection that I enjoyed, I adopted a somewhat reserved attitude vis-à-vis that principle.

I did not find the arguments convincing.

As a term paper in the seminary, a term paper that was a necessary condition for obtaining the licenciate, I chose the subject of St. Thomas Aquinas's teaching on the law of nations. My purpose was to show that for St. Thomas the law of nations was not the same as what is called "natural law," but rather a part of positive law. In consequence, St. Thomas was not saying that private property was a matter of natural law, but simply of positive law (the law of nations). I believe that I developed this study with considerable methodological precision, and that my conclusion was established in a sufficiently solid way.

From that time onward I always carried with me, even if not clearly formulated, the intuition that the teaching of the Church's magisterium on the right to private ownership of the means of production linked the Church powerfully to capitalism and placed it in a radical confrontation with socialism (over an issue that had nothing to do with the faith), thus forcing the Church to serve the cause of social conservatism and placing it in opposition to the longings of the oppressed to be freed.

This attitude remained more or less unchanged until 1947, when—having completed the examinations for a doctorate in philosophy in Rome's Gregorian University—I began to teach ethics to the third-year class of the Jesuit College of Philosophy, then located in Madrid.

My duties as a professor of ethics forced me once again to study the problem of the Church's teaching on private property.

I began to acquire one new insight after another, aided by students who threw themselves enthusiastically into a seminar on ethics under my supervision.

I was able to develop additional evidence that the major Scholastics of the sixteenth century and first half of the seventeenth had taught that private property was established by positive law, not by natural law.

I later discovered that the starting point for evaluating private property, as the issue arose for medieval theologians, was that a community of property of one kind or another is demanded by natural law. Since these theologians accepted the system of property that existed in their world (in broad terms, feudalism based on landholding), their problem was to show that some kind of private property was admissible. This they attempted in many different ways.

The idea that a community of goods is demanded by natural law was a heritage passed on to medieval theology from the Fathers of the Church through St. Isidore of Seville (*Etymologiae* or *Origines*, 5, 4) and the Decretals of Gratian (first part, introduction, D. VIII).

Specifically, I succeeded in establishing for myself quite clearly that the Fathers of the Church constantly and unanimously insisted that a community of goods is the basic principle of the social and economic order of creation: God made material things for all men. They also stated repeatedly that the accumulation of wealth is the fruit of robbery. They did not condemn private property absolutely, provided it was used justly. They did not attempt any analysis of economic and social structures, nor did they anticipate the possibility of qualitative change of these structures. In consequence, as a just use of wealth and as a factor in the achievement of social justice, the only device they offered was almsgiving. But they constantly insisted that the duty of giving alms was an obligation "of justice."

The idea that private ownership of the means of production is demanded by the natural law is foreign to the thought of the Church Fathers.

Dr. Restituto Sierra Bravo published, in 1967, a lengthy manual on the social and economic teaching of the Fathers of the

Church.[10] His purpose in this work was to discover possible exaggerations in the interpretation of the viewpoints of the Fathers. With this in mind, I have found only four texts that speak of the "necessity" of private property, two of Clement of Alexandria (No. 69 and No. 92 in Sierra Bravo's book), one of Theodoret of Syria (No. 1184), and one of St. Epiphanius (No. 1220).

Of these, the first text of Clement and that of Epiphanius are limited to defending the lawfulness of private property against heretics who called for a community of property and of wives. Clement's second text defends the lawfulness of private property to the extent that it may be necessary for providing the necessities of life, and he insists on the duty of almsgiving. Besides, Clement is one of those who stress most insistently the idea of a fundamental community of goods. "God established our nature for mutual communion, beginning himself by communicating his own things and by providing for all men his own Word (*logos*), making all things for all men. All things, in consequence, are common and the rich have no right to any advantage. The common saying, therefore, that goes "I have all I need and more, so why shouldn't I enjoy it" is neither human nor neighborly; more friendly is the other saying—"I have, then why should I not share with those in need?"[11]

Regrettably the only dissenting text is that of Theodoret (first half of the fifth century). He insists on the need for class inequality, so that the dispossessed will have no choice but to work in manual labor. Theodoret anticipates here, in a lower key, the dialectic of master and slave. But his voice is not enough to break the unanimity of outlook of the Fathers of the Church.

I set out the results of my study of the issue of property in the Church Fathers in a talk I gave in Barcelona on April 16, 1962 (published in my already mentioned work, *Christian Attitudes to Social Problems* [Barcelona, 1967], pp. 9–43).

---

[10] *Doctrina social y económica de los Padres de la Iglesia.* Colección general de documentos y textos (Madrid, 1967).
[11] *Pedagogus*, 2, 12; Stählin edition, I, 229.

From 1961 onward, in my courses on "The Social Teaching of the Church" in the Institute of Social Sciences of the Gregorian University, Rome, I continued to deal with the issue of material goods in the light of the New Testament.

In the 1969–70 course I finally reached a firm synthesis on this subject. In addition to my study and reflection over the years, I had occasion during that scholastic year to read Hans Joachim Dagenhardt's thesis on St. Luke[12] as the evangelist of the poor. This book helped me.

The fundamental principle of the New Testament regarding material goods (of the attitude of the Christian in dealing with material goods) is the principle of *koinonía* (the community of goods).

We find this principle formulated in the descriptions of the first Christian community presented in the Acts of the Apostles (2:42, 44, 45; 4:32, 34, 35). Luke says of the first Christian community that it remained faithful to the *koinonía*, that is, to the community of goods; that the faithful "owned everything in common"; that they shared their goods "according to what each one needed"; that "the whole group of believers was united, heart and soul; no one claimed for his own use anything he had, as everything they owned was held in common"; that "none of their members was ever in want," because their resources were "distributed to any members who might be in need."

It is quite clear that Luke was here concerned, not so much with telling the story of the first Christian community, as with setting forth an ethicoprophetic principle, a value indicator: the community of goods and the rule of "to each according to his needs."

In a lecture I delivered at Assisi on December 30, 1967, I referred in the following terms to these passages from the Acts of the Apostles:

To get a clear perspective on this question, which is of basic importance for the Christian life, I wish to bring to your attention the very earliest kind of religious instruction used in apostolic

---

[12] Hans Joachim Dagenhardt, *Lukas Evangelist der Armen* (Stuttgart, 1965).

times, as it has been preserved for us in the first chapters of the Acts of the Apostles. Of particular interest is Peter's talk to the group who had been attracted by the miracle of Pentecost (Ac. 2:14-36), and also his comments on the same miraculous happenings to the people (Ac. 3:12-26) and to the Jewish rulers, elders, and scribes (4:8-12) regarding the cure of the cripple at the Temple gate.

I see in these texts of Luke an element that I regard as important as a starting point. The essential components of the apostolic religious instruction are these: the coming of Jesus of Nazareth from God, his redeeming death on the cross, his glorification, and the gift of the Holy Spirit. It is important to note that in both these texts, Luke joins this summary of the essential components of the apostolic religious instruction with a description of that first experience of Christian life of the original community (Ac. 2:42 and 44-45; 4:32 and 34-35): They had a "community" (*koinonía*) of hearts and of goods, and no one was in need, because the goods of all were available for the needs of all.

Here we have something that is very important. Our salvation is the living Christ. It does not consist in the enunciation of the four points of the religious instruction (incarnation, crucifixion, resurrection, and ascension), but in a living faith in the living Christ. It is a faith that is an incorporation and also salvation, and that becomes real in the gift of the Spirit. Cornelius and his household listened with their hearts to Peter's proclamation, and hearing it, they received the Holy Spirit (Ac. 10:44). But the gift of the Holy Spirit is inseparable from that *koinonía* of hearts and goods that is the sign and fruit of the Spirit, as presented in the first epiphany of Pentecost. This is something we cannot doubt if we want to remain faithful to the message of Luke. . . .

Here we are contemplating a profound truth. Christianity, as lived life, is love of the brotherhood and is "community of hearts and goods" (*koinonía*). Obviously, this affirmation of the earliest *kerigma* (proclamation)—the community of goods—is not an affirmation of a juridic character. It is not the promulgation of a Christian law proscribing private property in legal form. The call for a "community" of hearts and goods is an ethicoreligious one, but it is an effective one. There is no Christianity without a community of hearts, and there is no community of hearts without an effective community of goods. The New Testament does not give us a legal model of state law. But it does give us an authoritative religious norm: "You are to live in communion with your neighbor in all things and you are not to say that anything is exclusively yours; because if you are sharers together in the things that are incorruptible, how much more in corruptible things?" That statement can be found, in the same exact words, in two extremely old records (first half of the second century), the so-called Letter of Bernabe (probably of Alexandrian origin) and the Didache (probably from Syria). The words undoubtedly come from an earlier source, which can be considered the oldest Christian work of the apostolic era. That confers an enormous importance on the document and helps us to understand the normative value of Luke's descriptions.

Two further references to the *koinonía* are found in the Letter to the Hebrews and in a passage of the second Letter of St. Paul to the Corinthians.

The Letter to the Hebrews (13:16) urges Christians to "keep doing good works and sharing your resources (*koinonía*), for these are sacrifices that please God."

Paul's message to the Corinthians is particularly important, because it shows us that the principle of sharing of resources (*koinonía*) is always valid, even if the social circumstances and the way to apply it may change. Paul is not thinking of a sale of one's capital goods in order to distribute the money received for them and use it to take care of the needs of all the members. He is referring rather to a practice of putting all income in a common purse so that each shares with the other according to his needs. But the principle of sharing of resources (*koinonía*) still stands.

In the context, Paul urges the Corinthians to contribute generously to the collection for the Jerusalem community. Then he adds: "As long as the readiness is there, a man is acceptable with whatever he can afford; never mind what is beyond his means. This does not mean that to give relief to others you ought to make things difficult for yourselves: It is a question of balancing what happens to be your surplus now against their present need, and one day they may have something to spare that will supply your own need. That is how we strike a balance." (II Co. 8:12–14).

Here it becomes clear how the full meaning of the Christian life and of the community of faith of Christians comes into play in the community of goods (in the efficacious realization of the principle of *koinonía*).

In the Letter to the Romans, Paul further says that the Christian communities of gentile origin had the duty of collecting help for the poor of the Christian community of Jerusalem, because they had received the spiritual benefits of the faith from that community (Rm. 15:26–27). The perspective is different in the second Letter to the Corinthians that we have been considering: Here the fact of having helped those in need will constitute the ground for freeing them from being abandoned when they face God's judgment. This is a thought that is forcibly stressed in St. Luke's Gospel (14:12–14; 16:9), and particularly in the parable of the last judgment in St. Matthew's Gospel (25:31–46).

On this parable, I wrote in 1967, in my book, *Christian Attitudes to Social Problems* (pp. 207–8):

The "meaning" of Christian "existence" is faith, in the sense of lived truth by virtue of love, and the personal working of justice with a social dimension is essential to this kind of love. This final "meaning" of the Christian life emerges with striking clarity in the parable in which Jesus described the final judgment, as recounted by St. Matthew (Mt. 25:31–46). The judgment on human existence, that is to say, the manifestation of its inner meaning, which has been realized by the virtuous and betrayed by the evildoers, is concerned exclusively—in the parable—with the dynamism of a love that actually succeeds in working justice, giving food to the hungry, drink to the thirsty, welcome to the stranger, clothing to the naked, comfort to the sick, and care to the prisoner. These acts of identification with our neighbors and of human and social justice are what give it final and definitive meaning in the eyes of God to human existence. However—and here is an essential aspect of this teaching of Jesus Christ—while these acts at the level of appearances pertain to the temporal order, they achieve the very highest religious dimension, the immediate personal relationship with Christ, who is our only way to God. That is the originality of the teaching of Jesus in this prophetic discourse on God's judgment. The idea that God rewards works of mercy in favor of those in need is already present both in rabbinical literature and in Egyptian wisdom. But Jesus here reveals an incomparably more profound mystery, that of his own real identification with the needy and the oppressed, as well as the reality of the highest possible form of religious encounter with him when we lovingly practice justice and mercy toward the destitute. This is made clear by the astonishment of those rewarded and those punished alike by the sentence. That astonishment is graphically portrayed by the bewildered question: "Then the virtuous will say to him in reply, 'Lord, when did we see you hungry and feed you; or thirsty and give you drink? When did we see you a stranger and make you welcome; naked and clothe you; sick or in prison and go to see you?' And the King will answer, 'I tell you solemnly, insofar as you did this to one of the least of these brothers of mine, you did it to me.' . . . Then it will be their turn to ask, 'Lord, when did we see you hungry or thirsty, a stranger or naked, sick or in prison, and did not come to your help?' Then he will answer, 'I tell you solemnly, insofar as you neglected to do this to one of the least of these, you neglected to do it to me.'" (Mt. 25:37–40 and 44–45).

In addition to establishing the fundamental character of the principle of the sharing of resources (*koinonía*), the New Testament gives us other points of reference regarding the problem of private ownership of wealth:

The possession of private wealth is a danger to the Christian life and to the attitude of openness to the Kingdom of God that Jesus preached. This comes out clearly in the version of the Beatitudes found in St. Luke: "How happy are you who are poor: Yours is the kingdom of God. Happy you who are hungry now: You shall be satisfied. Happy you who weep now: You shall laugh." Then come the contrasting parallels: "But alas for you who are rich: You are having your consolation now. Alas for you who have your fill now: You shall go hungry. Alas for you who laugh now: You shall mourn and weep." (Lk. 6:20–21 and

24–25). The stress is somewhat different in St. Matthew (5:3, 6), but there is no contradiction between the two versions. It is significant that Matthew is the only evangelist to preserve for us the parable of the Last Judgment that stresses that the realization in action of the *koinonía* or sharing of resources is the key issue in the last analysis for the "salvation" (the achievement) of human existence.

That Jesus placed us on guard against the danger inherent in private ownership of wealth is stated clearly in all three synoptic Gospels. Here is St. Mark's version of a striking statement that the Catholic Church has ignored *in practice* for centuries:

Jesus looked around and said to his disciples, "How hard it is for those who have riches to enter the kingdom of God!" The disciples were astounded by these words, but Jesus insisted, "My children," he said to them, "how hard it is to enter the kingdom of God! It is easier for a camel to pass through the eye of a needle than for a rich man to enter the kingdom of God." They were more astonished than ever. "In that case," they said to one another, "who can be saved?" Jesus gazed at them. "For men," he said, "it is impossible, but not for God: because everything is possible for God." (Mk. 10:23–27).

It is possible, nevertheless, to overcome the danger inherent in wealth. In St. Luke's Gospel (9:1–9) we find the story of Zacchaeus, whom Jesus declared to be "a son of Abraham." But that was only after Zacchaeus had decided to give half of his goods to the poor and undertaken to make fourfold restitution to anyone he might have cheated.

According to the New Testament, it is not possible to enter the Kingdom without an effective sharing of resources (*koinonía*), and that is incompatible with rigid class structures based on the accumulation of private wealth.

The fundamental point is the incompatibility between greed for money and Christianity. Luke (16:13) and Matthew (6:24) have handed on to us some phrases that constitute a condemnation of our so-called "Christian Western civilization." They say:

"No one can be the slave of two masters: He will either hate the first and love the second, or treat the first with respect and the second with scorn. You cannot be the slave both of God and of money."

The Letters of St. Paul to the Colossians (3:5) and to the Ephesians (5:5) tell us that greed is "idolatry" and that the greedy man is an idolater.

Finally, the first Letter to Timothy, in a text I already mentioned (6:5–10), offers us the Christian ideal of *autárkeia* (contentment), which is correlative to *koinonía*.

Here is the text: "Religion, of course, does bring large profits, but only to those who are content with what they have. We brought nothing into the world, and we can take nothing out of it; but as long as we have food and clothing, let us be content with that. People who long to be rich are a prey to temptation." (I Tm. 6:6–9).

In my talk at Assisi (December 30, 1967) on Christians and revolution, I commented briefly in these terms on that text:

The word *autárkeia* is interesting, more than anything else, in this text. This word has a very rich meaning, as is suggested by the derived word "autarky" in modern languages.

In the Pauline text under discussion, the word *autárkeia* has simultaneously two distinct meanings. It signifies, on the one hand, "a sufficiency of goods," what one might call in contemporary language, a human standard of living. The same word *autárkeia* is used in this first sense elsewhere by St. Paul, namely, in his second Letter to the Corinthians (9:8). But in the passage from the first Letter to Timothy that we are examining, *autárkeia* means *also* "to be content with what we have and not seek more."

The meaning of *autárkeia* presented here as a substantive element in the ideal of the Christian life is this. *We should try to establish for ourselves a truly human living level and be content with that, excluding the attitude of unlimited "desire" to "have more."* St. Paul makes this clear in the most precise terms, as mentioned above: "As long as we have food and clothing, let us be content with that." And immediately afterward, in the most explicit manner and with the greatest possible emphasis, he condemns the desire of unlimited wealth: "People who long to be rich are a prey to temptation; they get trapped into all sorts of foolishness and dangerous ambitions, which eventually plunge them into ruin and destruction. The love of money is the root of all evils." (I Tm. 6:9-10).

This scriptural text presents the Christian conscience with a really serious problem. And it seems to me that one of the most typical manifestations of the seriousness of the situation (of the inner meaning of the "crisis") in which Christians today find themselves is the fact that—for nearly two centuries—we have shown so little awareness of this problem.

What is at issue is the radical opposition between the "spirit" of capitalism (of the basic "ideology" of capitalism) and the teachings of Scripture, that is to say, the Word of God. The reason is that modern capitalism is built on the denial of *autárkeia* (contentment) and an enthusiastic commitment to the unrestricted desire of gain, to the uncontrolled longing to "have" each day more "things" than the day before.

In St. Paul, this ideal (value) of *autárkeia* is linked with the value of work as service, and it has a marked social dimension.

I dealt with the Pauline teaching on work (human, professional) and its value in the life of the Christian in a book published in French in 1965 and in Spanish in 1969.[13]

I continued to study the matter and reflect further on it in relation to the problem of worker-priests, and on other occasions.

In the 1965 book just mentioned, I synthesized Paul's thought, as follows:

Paul's teaching in his two Letters to the faithful of Thessalonika concerning the relationship between professional work and the perfection of love may be summed up in this way. The perfection

[13] Spanish title: *La perfección de la caridad y la actividad económica y social* (the perfection of love and economic and social activity) (Barcelona: Herder, 1969), in the collection *Santidad y vida en el siglo* (holiness and life in the world). The French edition was published by Herder in Rome, 1965.

The Pauline texts are found in the first Letter to the Thessalonians (4:9-12), the second Letter to the Thessalonians (3:6-15), his address to the elders of the church of Ephesus (Ac. 20:33-35), the Letter to the Ephesians (4:28), and the first Letter to Timothy (6:17-19).

of love is inseparable from a spirit of identification with others and of service, and that spirit cannot coexist with a situation in which one gets the benefit of the work of others without giving them the benefit of his own services in return. . . .

Paul's viewpoint is set forth with total clarity in his talk to the elders of the church of Ephesus who had assembled at Miletus to say farewell to him as he set out for Jerusalem: "I have never asked anyone for money or clothes; you know for yourselves that the work I did earned enough to meet my needs and those of my companions. I did this to show you that this is how we must exert ourselves to support the weak, remembering the words of the Lord Jesus, who himself said, "There is more happiness in giving than in receiving." (Ac. 20:33–35).

This striking text brings us once more to the two Letters to the Thessalonians. As we have seen, St. Paul expressed in them his disapproval of those who live in idleness and sustain themselves on the work of others. He is not here talking about the idle rich who live on their unearned income, because this class did not exist among the Christians of Thessalonika. But his teaching should be extended to every Christian. The rich man who lives in idleness is a burden to others. Even if his situation is not the same on the individualistic micro-economic level as that of the poor man who eats at the expense of another (since the idle rich man is paying those who work for him), he is certainly a parasite on the social and community level, in the sense that he benefits from the common effort without contributing his own activity to the common effort (work), which is necessary in order that all may live.

I tried to bring together in a fuller synthesis my views on the problem of the Christian ideal (value and duty) of work in a book I published in 1966.[14]

The duty of work, in a spirit of recognition of our social community of responsibilities and interests, applies equally in St. Paul's thought to the rich and the poor. In the first Letter to Timothy, written in the last years of his life, perhaps when rich members were becoming less infrequent in the Christian communities, Paul wrote these words: "Warn those who are rich in this world's goods that they are not to look down on other people;

14 *Lavoro, carità e giustizia* (work, love, and justice) (Assisi, 1966), a contribution to the collection *Laici sulla via del Concilio* (laity on the road of the Council).

and not to set their hopes on money, which is untrustworthy, but on God who, out of his riches, gives us all that we need for our happiness. Tell them that they are to do good, and be rich in good works, to be generous and willing to share—this is the way they can save up a good capital sum for the future if they want to make sure of the only life that is real." (I Tm. 6:17–19). In this text, "to do good" does not mean "to be willing to share" (this is a separate obligation added to the former). What it means above all is to work personally for the benefit of others (in an unselfish spirit), so as to become "rich in good works." To do good is, as it is so well expressed in the Letter to the Ephesians, "to find some useful manual work . . . and be able to do some good by helping others that are in need" (Ep. 4:28). The same expression, "to do good," is used in a sermon of St. Paul preserved in the Acts of the Apostles to indicate the beneficent action of God: "he sends you rain from heaven, he makes your crops grow when they should, he gives you food and makes you happy" (Ac. 14:16).

Paul's concept, which is rooted in the religious and cultural tradition of the Bible and of Semitic thought, is that of a spirituality of work. The Greco-Roman idea was that of refined and aristocratic "idleness" supported by a slave-based civilization. Professional and income-producing work is the function of the "slaves." Literary "idleness" is the proper activity of the "masters." Most "liberal" occupations, indeed! On this issue, the Christian has been perverted by his contact with Greco-Roman classicism. We must get back to the biblical sources, to Paul and the Prophet and even more pertinently, draw closer to Christ (the Son of God), who was identified both juridically and socially while on earth as "the carpenter's son" (Mt. 13:55), and also by himself as "the carpenter, the son of Mary" (Mk. 6:3).

St. Paul conceives of humanity as a great brotherhood of workers bound together by chains of common interests and concerns. In consequence, anyone who does not work when able to ("the man who will not work," St. Paul says expressly) lives at the expense of his fellows, because he is a part of a great working community (work being the vocation of mankind from the beginning) and benefits from the goods of that community without giving his contribution of work as a committed member to the common purpose. In St. Paul's view, this implies that the rich must work in the same way as the poor.

It is well known that St. Paul did not raise the issue of slavery as an institution. To raise that issue was beyond the concrete possibilities of the early Church in the historical and sociological situation of that time. But Paul, by formulating radical spiritual and religious demands in the area of master-slave relations, laid the base for further progress. Christians, on the contrary, throughout their entire history, have been very unfaithful to the spirit of Paul, which was a faithful reflection of that of Christ. In St. Paul's view, master and slave are equally obligated to work with a religious spirit in the service of their neighbor, who is a member of Christ. "Slaves, be obedient to the men who are called your masters in this world, with deep respect and sincere loyalty, as you are obedient to Christ; not only when you are under their eye, as if you had only to please men, but because you are slaves of Christ and wholeheartedly do the will of God. Work hard and willingly, but do it for the sake of the Lord and not for the sake of men. You can be sure that everyone, whether a slave or a free man, will be properly rewarded by the Lord for whatever work he has done well. And those of you who are employers, treat your slaves in the same spirit; do without threats, remembering that they and you have the same Master in heaven and he is not impressed by one person more than by another." (Ep. 6:5–9). Paul expresses this same idea (masters and slaves truly united as brothers, coworkers in the service of the brotherhood) with inimitable conciseness in the Letter to the Galatians: "Serve one another in works of love." (Ga. 5:13). He is here very much in line with the prophet Zephaniah in his description of the community in the time of the Messiah (Zp. 3:11–13).

I have thought it proper to dwell at some considerable length on the reflections derived from my studies of the New Testament as it bears on the relationship of Christianity to money. I have done this because I had myself to travel the same long road in order to free myself from the tremendous burden imposed on my conscience as a Catholic by the assertion of the papal magisterium that private ownership of the means of production is "a natural right." That assertion was derived from the middle-class liberalism of the nineteenth century, not from any genuine Christian tradition. In the last analysis, and speaking frankly, it was a false assertion.

For as long as I can remember, I always tried to interpret the teaching of the papal magisterium on private property as broadly as possible, stressing the more positive and less conservative statements, and trying to get above the collusion that objectively existed—in the concrete, historical dialectic—between the so-called social teaching of the Church (the papal magisterium of the nineteenth century) and the defense of the capitalist system against socialism. This defense of capitalism has been (and still is in large part) an historic fact, in spite of some verbal criticisms of capitalism.

The promulgation by the Second Vatican Council of the Pastoral Constitution on the Church in the Modern World (*Gaudium et spes*), in which—finally!—the unfortunate assertion that private ownership of the means of production is "a natural right" was abandoned, opened the way for me to carry my analysis a step farther. I did this in my 1967 book (already mentioned) on Christian attitudes to social problems, and in a more developed form in a paper presented at the Third National Congress of Italian Moralists, in Padua, March 31 to April 4, 1970.

My approach was to stress that the underlying intention of the statement by the magisterium, when it said that private ownership of the means of production was "a natural right," was to proclaim that every man should have a truly personal participation in the ownership of goods, and that in consequence totalitarian, dictatorial and bureaucratic forms of state ownership are not acceptable. But at the same time, I brought out the antichristian cultural conditionings that had affected the teaching of the Popes, the defective manner of formulating the issue, the ambiguities and (though this I had to say in somewhat veiled words) the possible elements of error in a strict sense.

Today, in this confession of my faith as a Christian, I want to say the same things in simpler and clearer words.

The teaching of the New Testament does not give us a social-economic or juridical-political organizational formula concerning the ownership of goods, and specifically of the means of production.

However, in the present moment of historic evolution, the "road to socialism" (leaving open all the issues that have to be left open) represents a possibility of organizing "the city of man" in a way that is not in opposition to the great evangelical values of *koinonía*, brotherhood (*agape*), *autárkeia*, and work faithful to a spirit of other-directed social service.

Capitalism (in spite of its kaleidoscopic ability to come up with all sorts of so-called "new" forms) does not offer the same possibility.

And in this historic situation, the defense of private ownership of the means of production by the Catholic Church, notwithstanding certain claims or pretenses to be defending "another kind" of private property quite different from that which now exists, constitutes in the objective order a very powerful support for the liberal bourgeois ownership of contemporary capitalism.

It is true that, since the Second Vatican Council, the official magisterium no longer proclaims private ownership of the means of production to be a natural right. Its new position, nevertheless, falls far short of a clean break. The Catholic Church as a whole (and in the whole of its "apparatus") has not yet laid aside an instinctive deep-seated "antisocialism," which is not Christian but rather middle-class antichristian. It cannot disguise as zeal for God's cause an attitude that comes to a far greater extent from concern for money, when Jesus has told us that a Christian cannot serve money.

A Christian who has succeeded in seeing or in sensing these facts cannot fail to feel himself free, vis-à-vis the establishment of his Church, in this area, and seek to move forward in history, in the light of the Gospel.

For my own part, I took a modest stand—for my possibilities are modest—but a clear one when I made a statement at the Valleumbrosa Study Congress on August 28, 1970:

97

The Christian community was guilty of a social and historic sin in the nineteenth century: It accepted the liberal bourgeois concept of individualistic private property as the basis of the social, economic, and political order. The assertion that private ownership of the means of production is "a natural right" introduced into the social teaching of the Church a misunderstanding [here—I add today—the literary procedure of the euphemism still comes somewhat into play] that prevented the Christian community to withdraw from the social sin of the nineteenth century.

It is necessary to say in clear terms:

1. That private ownership of the means of production is not a matter of "natural right."

2. That a system of ownership that is not truly social is incompatible with Christianity.

3. That state ownership of the means of production need not be "social."

4. That it seems impossible (or at least very difficult) for a system of ownership of the means of production that is predominantly private to be simultaneously truly "social."

I repeated these statements in a lecture I gave in Oviedo on October 8 of the same year, 1970, with the following additions:

This brings us to the issue of socialism.

The notion of socialism has more than a single meaning. In consequence, when we speak of socialism [and this applies also to Marxist or Marxian socialism, I add today, in order to avoid misunderstandings] we have to see what it is we are talking about.

One can speak of socialism in the sense of an economic and social order based not on the private ownership of the means of production, but on other kinds of collective ownership, which ensure on the one hand the participation of the workers in the management of the means of production, and which on the other hand avoid an authoritarian and unchecked ownership by a state bureaucracy over the economy, thus ensuring the participation of the citizens in the fundamental planning options.

If we admit, as I think we must (if we study the facts without prejudice), that it seems impossible in practice for a predominantly private system of ownership of the means of production to be authentically "social," then we must agree that the structure of society has to be fundamentally socialist, in the sense just presented of a socialism "with a human face." How can this be effected? We will need to work competently and imaginatively, and also with determination. I believe that the sincere Christian who has not been perverted by historic conditionings (for which he may not be personally to blame) will be eager for a turn of the rudder in the direction of socialism.

A more complex problem would be the following. Should we accept a systematic and total (absolute) abolition of every kind of private ownership of the means of production?

Dogmatism is likely to be dangerous. And I believe that it would be in opposition to the underlying intention of "scientific socialism."

Christian principles as such do not include directly the need for a complete abolition of the private ownership of the means of production. But a proposal of this kind could be the result of an analysis of historical reality. A Christian or a group of Christians could come to this conclusion without impairment of their commitment to Christianity. In fact, the complete abolition of private ownership of the means of production is not opposed in itself either to Christian principles or to so-called natural law, as long as we respect the principle of the primacy of man [I add today: a principle that capitalism—because of its intimate structure—is incapable of respecting, and that socialism is able to respect] and avoid the excesses of dictatorial, bureaucratic, and uncontrollable centralized power. The Church, therefore, could not condemn such a political and social option on the ground that it was protecting Christian values.

And yet it has done just that. The teaching of the magisterium on private property (for decades and decades) and its stand in the historic dialectic between capitalism and socialism represent a degeneration when compared with the Gospel values concerning the goods of this world. How has that come about?

It has come about because the ecclesiastical "apparatus," from way back, has made deals with the rich and powerful, betraying the message of the Kingdom of God. It has offered the rich a modified version of the Gospel, expurgating such statements as "Woe to you who are rich," and "It is easier for a camel to pass through the eye of a needle than for a rich man to enter the

Kingdom of God." In return, it has been coopted as a participant in wealth and power. And it has established—and this also inside the Church itself—a human system of power resembling far too closely the dialectic of "master" and "slave."

It came as a real surprise to find in so eminent a scripture scholar and so committed a Christian as the German exegete, Joaquin Jeremias, the incredible statement that "Jesus does not attempt to take a stand on the problem of rich and poor."[15] Equally astonishing is his picturesque interpretation that the "friends" we have to make by giving alms to the needy, as stated by St. Luke (16:2), may well be angels, because the reference cannot be to the poor.[16]

Precisely because of the esteem in which I hold Joaquin Jeremias, a man who has helped me greatly in my efforts to understand the Gospels, this unexpected and incredible lapse seems to me symptomatic. Here this excellent exegete (a Protestant) is the victim of the conditioning that he received from his church, a conditioning exactly the same as that which we Catholics get from our own church.

It is not true that Jesus does not attempt to take a stand on the problem of rich and poor. It is the great Christian churches that do not want to take a stand, because they have joined the rich. Because of that, they pretend that *they take no position* (at the verbal level), so that they can remain, historically and in fact, in an alliance with the rich in the war of the rich against the poor. This fact makes it necessary to empty of all meaning the "good news for the poor" that the Gospel is, transforming it into a "spiritual" statement that will not disturb the rich.

In the Catholic Church, the problem of "wealth" and "power" constitutes a kind of structural unity. Churchmen believe (many of them in good faith) that they cannot exercise the pastoral

[15] The author's references are to a French translation, 1962, *Les paraboles de Jésus*, p. 175, of a German original. The book is also in English: *The Parables of Jesus* (New York: Scribners, 1955).
[16] *Ibid.*, pp. 51 and 52 (note 12).

office without a human platform of "power." To maintain that platform, they need money. But in order to have money, they end up by rejecting "the Gospel for the poor," which was that of Jesus.

If we returned to the Gospel and abandoned the fetishism of "money power," perhaps we would find that we have solved structural problems of the Church that seem today to have us completely boxed in.

As an illustration, I would end here with a paradoxical thought, humorous perhaps but also significant, which I have offered in friendly conversations in recent years, and which continues to stimulate my mind.

How should the primacy of the Pope function in the contemporary world? At what level of "power" should it be exercised?

The question is a thorny one. The Vatican tends to think, we can presume in all good faith, that all of the power and centralization that it now possesses (and that it seeks jealously to retain even though it has begun inexorably to slip from its grasp) belongs to it "by divine right."

The younger generations do not accept that kind of notion and structure of "power."

Many ecumenists believe that a major change is needed in the concrete way in which the "primacy" is understood and exercised.

Theological discussions seem unable to answer the question.

Would it be possible to try a way that would be simultaneously more evangelical and more pragmatic?

This would be my proposal. (Obviously, it is the proposal of an imbecile, of a man in his dotage.)

The first point I would make is a theoretical one, yet a proposition that even the most conservative theologians will accept. The Pope today has no greater primacy than St. Peter had. Some might argue that he has less. But everyone will agree that he does not have more.

Next I present an undeniable historical point. The historical and social expression of the primatial function in Peter was infinitely more discreet and modest than in a modern Pope, for example, Pius XII.

It is, of course, necessary to recognize, if one is to escape the charge of being unrealistic and of lacking "an historic sense," that a Pope of the twentieth century cannot be expected to exercise the "primacy" in precisely the same way as St. Peter exercised it, which practically meant that he "did not exercise it" at all.

Having established these solid premises, we can now attack the question. Between the level of "exercise of the primacy" of St. Peter and that of Pope Pius XII, there is such an astronomical distance that, without attempting to re-establish the minimalism of St. Peter literally, it would be possible to change qualitatively the maximalism of Pius XII.

But where are we to find the intermediate point that we can use as the new level?

Here I present my paradoxical proposal. The believer is entitled to laugh, provided he laughs lovingly.

Let us think for a moment—without evil and even without malice—about the much-discussed question of the accumulated wealth of the Holy See.

There is no way to determine how much it is. And that is already a long way from the evangelical norm.

Let us suppose that the capital sum is somewhere between five hundred million and a billion dollars. That is where the estimates place it.

That the successor of St. Peter, the fisherman, known since the Middle Ages as the "vicar" of Christ, should have capital in the amount of five hundred million dollars is unpleasant and disturbing. That condition is loaded down with consequences that do not work in favor of the possibility of authentically evangelical witness and freedom.

Yet it is said, on the other hand, that modern Popes are austere and spend the income derived from this capital exclusively to finance the exercise of the primacy, and that it falls far short of their needs.

This is where my paradoxical "twist" is applicable.

Why don't we start from the economic aspect in order to resolve the problem of the level today desirable in the "exercise" of the primacy (a certain equilibrium between Peter and Pius XII).

Let us be realists and not think of a Pope as poor as St. Peter (in the material sense) and dispossessed of all his staff.

But why should we not have the courage to cut the accumulation of capital to fifty million dollars?

A gesture like that of Zacchaeus from the contemporary papacy would perhaps be the only way to exercise a social magisterium of the Popes, since it would seem that words have all been used up.

Somebody would undoubtedly object that it is impossible to exercise the primacy with the income earned by fifty million dollars of capital.

My answer would be (of course, I am weak-minded, an imbecile): If the Pope were to limit himself to exercising the level of primacy that can be exercised on the economic base of the income from fifty million dollars, I am sure he would not be unfaithful to Christ or to St. Peter. We can be sure that whatever he would be unable to exercise for lack of a broader economic base is not "of divine right."

All the above is just a joker's dream. Perhaps, however, it is not entirely unworthy of the serious concern of a Christian who believes in Jesus.

Be that as it may, if it is desirable to conclude on a more serious note, let us do so with a text of St. James. The Apostle shows us in a striking way that the temptation to ally with the rich, to shunt the poor to one side, and thus to lose the truth of the Gospel, has been hiding in wait for the Christian community from the very earliest times.

My brothers, do not try to combine faith in Jesus Christ, our glorified Lord, with the making of distinctions between classes of people. Now suppose a man comes into your synagogue, beautifully dressed and with a gold ring on, and at the same time a poor man comes in, in shabby clothes, and you take notice of the well-dressed man, and say, "Come this way to the best seats"; then you tell the poor man, "Stand over there" or "You can sit on the floor by my footrest." Can't you see that you have used two different standards in your mind, and turned yourselves into judges, and corrupt judges at that?

Listen, my dear brothers: It was those who are poor according to the world that God chose, to be rich in faith and to be the heirs to the kingdom which he promised to those who love him. In spite of this, you have no respect for anybody who is poor. Isn't it always the rich who are against you? Isn't it always their doing when you are dragged before the court? Aren't they the ones who insult the honorable name to which you have been dedicated? Well, the right thing to do is to keep the supreme law of scripture: You must love your neighbor as yourself; but as soon as you make distinctions between classes of people, you are committing sin, and under condemnation for breaking the Law. . . .

Talk and behave like people who are going to be judged by the law of freedom, because there will be judgment without mercy for those who have not been merciful themselves, but the merciful need have no fear of judgment. [Jm. 2:1–9 and 12–13].

8. Demythologization and the Recovery of Hope

Now I COME to the central issue raised by my reflection on my faith.

If my Christian religion, the Christianity I live, is to be a true religion, it must be ethicoprophetic. In order, however, to be ethicoprophetic in the biblical and genuinely Christian sense, it has to be saturated with Messianic hope. And Messianic hope is hope within history and drawn from history.

We find this confirmed in the most emphatic way in the testimony of St. Paul concerning the faith of the apostolic communities in the resurrection of Jesus, as set forth in the first Letter to the Corinthians (Chapter 15). Written about the year 55, this letter is the most ancient testimony to the faith that we possess.

This enormously important passage of the New Testament contains, in addition to the witness to faith in the reality of the resurrection of Jesus, a witness to the meaning this faith of the Christians contained as faith in the victory of Christ over death and in the lordship of Christ over history.

Some of the Christians of Corinth, whom Paul was addressing, doubted that men had a prospect of rising again after they had died. A man belonging to Greek culture did not find it difficult to admit the "immortality of the soul," but it was hard for him to accept the resurrection, the reconstitution of man after he had died, the principal reason being his negative concept of matter. But there was also another reason, namely, his "circular" (pessimistic, fatalistic) notion of history. The idea of the immortality of a "separated" soul points to a "salvation" completely independent of existence and of historic destiny, whereas the idea of "resurrection" brings us to a solution of the problem of historic man and of his existence in its properly human sense. It is admittedly a transcendent solution, but it is not a solution unconnected with and removed from historic existence.

What Paul actually does is to present his reply in the perspective of some Christians, who on the one hand affirm the resurrection of Jesus, but who on the other deny or question our resurrection. And his reply is overwhelming. If there is no resurrection for us, then neither did Christ rise from the dead. And if Christ is not risen, our whole religion is false. St. Paul repeats his thesis with all the energy of which he is capable. Either Christ rose and we also will rise from the dead; or, if we are not to rise, then neither did Christ rise, and the whole of Christian faith is an empty illusion (I Co. 15:12-19).

For a modern Western man, Paul's formation of the issue is not logical. But St. Paul does not here claim to be establishing his position on the basis of logic. Rather, his thought is developed within a dialectic of faith. What exists in this connection between the already accomplished resurrection of Jesus (object of our faith) and our own future resurrection (object of our hope) is the affirmation of a bond of fellowship that forms the innermost substance of Christianity: Jesus was born, lived, died, and was raised from the dead *for us*. And this is a truth that for the believer has a depth and a reality beyond all imagining.

The inseparable connection between the resurrection of Jesus and our resurrection represents also for St. Paul the unshakable affirmation that Jesus, the Christ, is actually the "Alpha and Omega" of the history of mankind in the universe. He later developed this idea enthusiastically in his Letter to the Romans. There he presented our resurrection as the liberating fulfillment of the history of the human race, and with it, of the entire dynamism or dialectic of "creation" (of the universe in which man historically lives) (Rm. 8:19–24).

If the resurrection of Jesus is not joined (as "first fruits") to our resurrection, and if our resurrection is not truly the fulfillment of history, then Jesus is not the Christ of God, the Christ for mankind and for history. But if Jesus is not the Christ, within this context, the resurrection of Jesus is a pure illusion and our Christianity is nothing more than a myth.

Such is the thought of St. Paul when he states and repeats that if there is no resurrection for us, neither can there have been for Jesus. But immediately afterward, Paul goes on to proclaim with all the energy he possesses that Christ Jesus has in fact risen from the dead: "But Christ has in fact been raised from the dead, the first fruits of all who have fallen asleep." (I Co. 15:20). He then explains that between the resurrection of Jesus, three days after the Pasch, and our resurrection, at the hour of the Second Coming of Jesus at the end of time, the whole course of human history will unfold. This history is seen by Paul as a function of the resurrection of Jesus, which is already a potential victory over evil and death: "All men will be brought to life in Christ; but all of them in their proper order: Christ as the first fruits and then, after the coming of Christ, those who belong to him. After that will come the end, when he hands over the kingdom to God the Father, having done away with every sovereignty, authority and power.

For he must be king until he has put all his enemies under his feet and the last of the enemies to be destroyed is death." (I Co. 15:22–26).

What do these words mean?

What Paul says is as follows. Jesus, having died and risen from the dead, receives an investiture, a kingdom, which has a dynamic meaning. The risen Christ is established as Lord so that he can carry out in history a process of subjugation of the powers of evil. Starting from the ideas then common among Jews about the function of angels in regard to men, St. Paul thinks of malevolent angelic powers, the activities of whom are evident in the observable patterns of evil in the course of history. It seems to me that it is quite immaterial (notwithstanding the contrary view of Oscar Cullmann) for the believer of today whether these powers have to be understood in a literal or a symbolic sense. What is important is that the subjugation of these "powers" is a real subjugation of evil and of structures supportive of wickedness in history and through history. This process, developing slowly but moving steadily toward victory, has as its crown the definitive triumph of life over death on the day of the coming of Jesus, which is the time of our resurrection.

The powers of evil of which St. Paul speaks represent all that is expressed as self-centeredness, oppression, injustice, and lack of love. (This is by contrast with the good, which for Paul—as we have seen—is identified with love, which works justice and does not work evil.) That evil has to be overcome, step by step, in the course of history. The mysterious Christ, Jesus who died and rose from the dead, is in a hidden way—because he remains in the mystery of the Father—a guarantee that the struggle has "meaning," and that it gives its "meaning" to history. This means that it not only has meaning in the existence of the individual who commits himself, for the sake of love, to the struggle against oppression (injustice), but that it also has meaning in history and with regard to the forward movement of history. All the forces of vicious interests, of conformism, of cowardice, and of historical pessimism, which try to smother every expression of challenge presented in the name of freedom and justice, will be powerless to eliminate from history the movement of resistance to selfishness, injustice, and oppression. That struggle, with all its historical complexities, with its uncertainties, its risks, and its periodic setbacks, is a dynamism on the march toward the end, toward the coming of Jesus, which will be the consummation and the definitive victory.

Such is Christian hope. Such is the content of faith in the resurrection of Jesus, the guarantee ("pledge") of our final resurrection.

I believe in this hope. And to proclaim my faith in this hope, I am writing this book.

It is against all those who, in the Church and outside it, try to convince us that we should reject hope in the name of prudence or common sense or science, or perhaps of a "supernatural spirit," which would be like saying "in the name of God."

What a mockery!

But let us return for a moment to St. Paul.

St. Paul sets up the following dialectic: 1. Christ has risen. 2. The struggle (with victory assured) against the powers of evil is in progress. 3. Linked to this struggle and to its victorious dynamism, is, as its crown, our resurrection.

Paul says specifically that it is not possible to believe with true faith in the resurrection of Jesus, unless we hope for (believe in) our own resurrection. But when he explains to us the dynamic relationship between the resurrection of Jesus and our resurrection, he inserts—as part of the activity proper to Christ—the entire web of history as a struggle against the powers of evil.

"The last of the enemies to be destroyed is death." In consequence, if the struggle against the enemies of brotherhood, of freedom, of true love, and of justice, is not a struggle on the road toward victory through the entire historical process, it is unrealistic to imagine that death is going to be conquered at the end.

We can thus set out fully the exact content of Paul's vision: If there is not a victorious struggle in process within history against the powers of evil, there is no resurrection for us. And if there is no resurrection for us, there is not and there has not been a resurrection of Jesus, and our Christianity is an illusion.

It is not possible to have a genuine faith in the resurrection without having an eschatological hope *related to history*, which *in consequence* cannot serve as an instrument of evasion.

Very many Christians, however, with their ontological-cultist outlook and their social conservatism, are tied functionally to a nonevangelical structure of clerical "power," and seem to have lost from sight the sense of hope. Paul's perspective, which is the expression of the faith of the Apostles in the resurrection, may seem to them a strangely new and questionable interpretation.

In spite of this, Paul's understanding of the dynamic link joining the resurrection of Jesus to the progressive subjugation of the "powers" of evil in history is not foreign to the view of the synoptic Gospels. The fact is that the authors of the synoptic Gospels were even closer than Paul himself to the Messianic perspective of the prophets of Israel. Mark is the evangelist of the imminent coming of the Kingdom, which is made manifest in Christ with paradoxical originality and sovereign freedom. And Luke stresses explicitly the connection between the Gospel of Jesus and biblical and Messianic hope: for example, in the two canticles, the Magnificat and the Benedictus (Lk. 1:46–55 and 68–79), in his curious account of the visit of Jesus to Nazareth (Lk. 4:16–21), and in the answer to the envoys of John the Baptist (Lk. 7:18–23), an episode also reported by St. Matthew (11:2–6).

St. Matthew's Gospel ends with these words:

"All authority on heaven and on earth has been given to me. . . . And know that I am with you always; yes, to the end of time." (Mt. 28:18 and 20).

This declaration is exactly the same as that made by St. Paul in his witness to faith in the resurrection:

"For he must be king until he has put all his enemies under his feet" and "After that will come the end, when he hands over the kingdom to God the Father, having done away with every sovereignty, authority and power." (I Co. 15:25 and 24).

The meaning of the above text of St. Matthew seems to me predominantly (if not exclusively) Messianic and eschatological, in the same line of thought as the Pauline concept of the risen Christ as Lord of history. But Catholics have left this meaning in the shade, searching instead for a legalistic notion of hierarchical "absolutism." That also should make us stop and think.

What is here and now important, however, is to face the most serious problem that presents itself to the Christian believer of our time.

First of all, it is necessary to recognize, on the one hand, that to retain the apostolic faith in the resurrection of Jesus is to retain the content of Messianic hope, the faith in Christ set up as the Lord of history; and these elements constitute the innermost substance of faith in the resurrection. Without this content of Messianic hope that acts in history, our belief in the resurrection become part of a myth, similar to the myths of the Dionysian mysteries (above all, as an "attitude" and as a religious "solution").

But is the way in which the Bible presents Messianic and eschatological hope to us not itself in turn mythological? And are there not also mythological elements in the way in which, after Jesus, the Christian faith of apostolic times resumed once more the old prophetic hope?

Is it possible for us to demythologize the Messianic hope, which is inseparable from genuine Christian belief in the resurrection, without losing that hope in the process, but instead—on the contrary—recovering it in a deeper sense in the process?

Personally I have done something of the sort. And I am conscious that it is only in this way that I have genuinely (as I hope) and in all its depth reached the true level of "faith."

I shall try to explain how I live my Messianic hope, my faith in the risen Christ, Lord of history.

But I first want to insist that this deepening of the faith (this demythologization), which carries us to the authentic level of naked "faith," and of the "hope," which is "believed," removes from us all apologetic pretense of "proving" our faith in order that others may thus accept it. Abraham "in hope believed against hope" (in the original Greek, *par' elpída ep' elpídi epísteusen*), St. Paul tells us in the Letter to the Romans (4:18). But such a "faith" in "hope," without any human support for the hope ("against hope"), is a kind of creation of grace inside a man, an original happening, an existential mystery.

The believer should carry with him his "faith in hope" by his total attitude rather than by his words. He should give testimony. But this he should do with extreme respect for others. He should avoid both proselytism and triumphalism. The reason is that he himself is conscious of the "folly," or perhaps better the "gratuity," of his hope. Yet this "folly" is lived by him as "the wisdom of God." And "the wisdom of God" frees a man from sectarianism and superstition, leaving him free to face reality in a spirit of sincerity, looking at it from the mystery of hope, but without mythologizing dogmatic presuppositions that would force him, in order to retain them, to close his eyes to the reality in front of him. For reality also is a mystery, and it has to be respected.

Against this background I shall try to explain how I demythologized and recovered my Messianic and eschatological hope, standing face to face with the reality of history.

The prophets of Israel hoped for the establishment of justice in the historic world, by means of an open and visible intervention of Yahweh, an intervention similar to that expressed in Israel's religious traditions about the exodus from Egypt and the miraculous passage through the Red Sea.

The new Moses referred to in Deuteronomy (18:15) was expected. He would be an offspring of David, and he would effect the liberation of the people directly and by the use of political means, as the Christ (the Anointed) of Yahweh. Such, for example, is the perspective of Psalm 72, in which the predictions—

sung, perhaps, for the crowning of a king—are deflected toward
the horizon of Messianic hope:

> God, give your own justice to the king,
>   your own righteousness to the royal son,
> so that he may rule your people rightly
>   and your poor with justice.
> Let the mountains and hills
>   bring a message of peace for the people.
> Uprightly he will defend the poorest,
> he will save the children of those in need,
>   and crush their oppressors.
> Like sun and moon he will endure,
>   age after age,
> welcome as rain that falls on the pasture,
>   and showers to thirsty soil.
> In his days virtue will flourish,
>   a universal peace till the moon is no more;
> his empire shall stretch from sea to sea,
>   from the river to the ends of the earth.
> The Beast will cower before him
>   and his enemies grovel in the dust;
> the kings of Tarshish and of the islands
>   will pay him tribute.
> The kings of Sheba and Seba
>   will offer gifts;
> all kings will do him homage,
>   all nations become his servants.
> He will free the poor man who calls to him,
>   and those who need help,
> he will have pity on the poor and feeble,
>   and save the lives of those in need;
> he will redeem their lives from exploitation and outrage,
>   their lives will be precious in his sight.
> Prayer will be offered for him constantly,
>   blessings invoked on him all day long.

Grain everywhere in the country,
  even on the mountain tops,
abundant as Lebanon its harvest,
  luxuriant as common grass!
Blessed be his name for ever,
  enduring as long as the son!
May every race in the world be blessed in him,
  and all the nations call him blessed!

There was a "mythological" element in this way of conceiving Messianic hope; and that mythological element must be eliminated, if the "myth" (a symbolic expression that can be a legitimate one) is not to be transformed into unsound "mythology" (a realistic, and consequently false, understanding of the "myth").

God does not intervene in history in the experiential and observable way in which the prophets of Israel described his actions in unsophisticated words.

The Gospel will, of course, always be meaningful for the Christian when it says: "Can you not buy five sparrows for two pennies? And yet not one is forgotten in God's sight. Why, every hair on your head has been counted. There is no need to be afraid: You are worth more than hundreds of sparrows." (Lk. 12:6–7, which is the same as Mt. 10:29–31). And the prayer of Jesus will also always have meaning: "Our Father . . . give us today our daily bread." (Mt. 6:9 and 11).

But this providence is to be understood as a mystery, not as a kind of factor that can enter into the calculation of the historic possibilities on the level of observation and experience.

If God's omnipotence is understood in terms of immediate intervention on the empirical level (a hair falls because God so willed decisively with a causal will on the empirical level), it is impossible to attribute to God the Father the goodness that Jesus made known about him. There is too much evil in the universe.

The "mediation" between creative omnipotence and the evolu-

113

tionary immanence of the universe or the dialectic of history is an absolute mystery.

God is for the believer the focus of hope, and we direct our prayer to him in the sense of mystery (the mystery of existence and the mystery of faith). We can even make allowance for the unforeseeable event, which can be lived by the believer on the religious plane of faith, as a "response" of God (by virtue of a charismatic "appeal" of the believer to God). Such "happenings" are located on that dividing line where empiric and observed reality (whether cosmic or historical) cannot be reduced to a simple determination of possibilities by scientific means. They are on that open "horizon" that prevents the full materialization of what is in fact "possible."

But that is something quite different from an understanding of providence that mixes up the immanent with the transcendent, transforming God into a chess player who moves the pieces on a cosmic chessboard.

It is much more in keeping with an authentic "faith" to say that we know nothing of the "way" in which omnipotence meshes with empirical reality.

Where the believer can see a possibility of direct intervention of the omnipotence of God in the existential occurrences of historic life is in the mystery of the heart of man. There the possibility does indeed exist of being touched by the hand of God. There is an opening to the possibilities of grace (*cháris*), of a "gift," of the breath of the Spirit.

But this pertains to the level of "the mystery of faith," which is beyond the level of possible analysis of depth psychology. Man, more than the universe, exists on a plane that is open to the impenetrable. The prayers and the hope of the believer are located at this opening.

As regards the political "mythologization" that the Messianic hope had undergone in the tradition of Israel, Jesus functioned during his historic life on earth as a "demythologizing" element.

This resulted from his vocation as a prophet and from his attitude to politics.

It seems to me that Oscar Cullmann is basically correct in the analysis he makes in his book on the relations of Jesus with contemporary revolutionaries.[17]

Jesus refused to become involved at the level of political action and in consequence disappointed the Zealots, who represented the survival of Messianic hope in its most political form and with a tendency to violent action.

Why did Jesus not formuate the political issue?

For two reasons. First, because his vocation was a prophetic one to the exclusion of all else, and because his idea of the Kingdom was rooted absolutely in personal conversion (*metanoia*), stressing the ethical purity of the Kingdom, which cannot be identified with the concrete expressions to be found at the political level. Second, because in all likelihood Jesus in his historical life shared the view, very common in his time and in his specific surroundings, that the Second Coming (*Parousia*) was very close at hand. In consequence, because the hour of final decision was so close at hand, there was time only for a radical decision at the personal level, not for political activity. Joaquin Jeremias is another who believes that all—or nearly all—the parables, in the original form in which they came from the lips of Jesus, reflected this viewpoint of the closeness of the end of the world.

But if Jesus was a "prophet" and not a "man of politics," this did not make him "apolitical." His ethicoprophetic attitude, when carried to its final conclusions, as well as his independence vis-à-vis the powerful of his time (and correlatively, his aggressiveness toward the rich), carried him to the point of confrontation. The outcome was that he found himself on trial in a Roman court and sentenced as a Zealot leader. There was in fact a partial identity of view between him and the Zealots, even if they moved on different planes.

[17] Oscar Cullmann, *Jesus and the Revolutionaries* (New York: Harper & Row, 1970).

The point that now interests me is this. The fact that Jesus did not enter directly into the political play of his historic time, together with the belief of the Christians of the apostolic era that he was in truth the Messiah, inevitably forced Christians to "demythologize" the directly political aspect that the work of the Messiah had assumed in the perspective of the prophets.

But this first "demythologization" in the New Testament was accompanied, as it seems to me, by a new kind of "mythologization," which has to be got rid of, without at the same time losing the essential content of the faith of the apostles.

The New Testament writers, perhaps in a way that is not unduly monolithic and with a variety of emphases, also undoubtedly shared the belief that the end of the world was at hand.

This fact, together with the splendor of the Spirit of Pentecost, which dazzled in a certain way the eyes of the first believers, caused them to think more or less along the following lines:

Jesus raised from the dead, the glorified Christ, Lord of history, is "already" the end of time. Simultaneously, however, he has to come again. His *Parousia* (Second Coming), which is the "fullness" of the end of time, is consequently awaited. This *Parousia* is close at hand. Between the resurrection and the pouring out of the Spirit, on the one side, and the *Parousia*, on the other, is "the time of the Church," which is nothing more than a continuation of the resurrection. The visible Church, as it exists in history, is the visible presence of the glorified Christ in history. It follows that the mediation of the Church, so understood, takes on a character of such essentiality and necessity that nothing else could take its place. It is only by explicit faith, historically existing and recognizable in the community of believers and in the empirical conscience of each believer, that the work of redemption can be effected. Only in and through this faith (or as a consequence of it) does the lordship of the glorified Christ over history move forward.

After years of reflection, of prayer, and of struggle to be sincere, I have reached the conviction that this view, which (to a greater or lesser extent) underlies the New Testament and conditions its language, includes a "mythological" element that has to be eliminated if we are not to lose the essential nucleus, valid for all time, that Christ is the only mediator and the only and universal redeemer.

I shall try to explain briefly how I live this faith in Christ as savior, and how—in spite of the unavoidable "demythologization" of the Church—the Church still continues on the plane of faith in Christ the redeemer.

The need for this "demythologization" arises from two directions. First is the recognition of the substantial failure of the Church as "a permanent epiphany" of the risen Christ in the world. The second is the realization that not only the historic life of Christ but also the historic life of the Church (the historic reality of the Christian communities) is something so insignificant (on the historical and empirical level) in comparison with the total flow of humanity from its origins to its final end, that if Christ is really the universal redeemer, his redemption is necessarily accomplished with great independence of any concrete mediation of an historic kind and is capable of being recognized and observed. Not only can the Church (understood in its historic existence as a social body) not be a necessary mediation, but neither can that quality be ascribed to the knowledge and "acknowledgment" of Christ in an explicit faith, the reality of which is historically identifiable and recognizable in the history of religions or of the churches.

The mystery of Christ's redemption is "a mystery of faith," as also is the "lordship" of Christ and "the history of salvation." To attempt to "incorporate" this mystery unduly in the Church that can be seen and in the faith that can be heard is to create a "mythology" and to compromise the absolute depth of the faith.

This does not mean that the Church that is seen and the faith that is heard do not belong to the mystery of Christ the Lord. It means rather that the mystery of Christ the Lord is far greater than the Church and than the community of those of us who conceive our faith explicitly and express it in words.

If the churches and we who are believers and witnesses are truly humble, what difficulty will we have in saying with John the Baptist: "He must grow greater, I must grow smaller." (Jn. 3:30)?

Contemporary theologians have explained that the drama of faith (the "call" of God, the "reply" of man) takes place far more in the depth of an option of conscience that chooses with the fullness of an "existential act" of *agape* (open love) instead of selfishness, than in the intellectual act of a "yes" of faith conceived and expressed conceptually and in the form of a "judgment."

In this existential option, made under the influence of a "grace" of which the recipient does not have to be conscious, there is existentially a "reply." It includes—before the moment of conceptualization—a "yes" of faith, not "spoken" but rather "lived."

One who is an atheist at the level of his concepts and his culture can be a believer at this existential depth. Everything depends on his attitude toward his neighbor.

This is the direction in which the parable of the good Samaritan seems to me to be pointing. For the Jews of the time of Jesus, a Samaritan was synonymous with being irreligious, a renegade, on the side of the devil. In spite of all that, the model Jesus offers of fulfillment of the law in authentic love of one's neighbor is the Samaritan who—without denying his "samaritanism" and going over to Jewish orthodoxy—is able to love his enemy truly. In the parable, the priest and the Levite are both disqualified (Lk. 10:25–37).

Just as a Samaritan could serve as a model for accepting the Kingdom of God at the time of Christ, so can an atheist today. And a priest who is fully orthodox can be left outside.

For me, who believes that Christ is the redeemer of mankind, an authentically live *agape* is always a "grace," always a mysterious identification with Christ, always the fruit of Jesus' self-surrender.

For this it is not necessary that a man should know (on the level of conceptualizable consciousness) God and Christ. What is here important is not that we should know God, but that God should "know" us, as St. Paul says (Rm. 8:29).

Some nonbelievers are annoyed by these attempts of contemporary theology to explain how the redeeming influence of Christ can extend beyond the limits of the Christian churches and beyond an explicit and professed Christian faith.

The reason for their annoyance is that they see in this step of modern theology a triumphalist effort on the part of the Church to "recover" the ground that it deservedly had lost.

My faith, however, contains no element of such triumphalism. On the contrary, it accentuates the smallness of the Church and the sovereign independence of the mystery of salvation in Christ.

Moreover, faith does not impose itself on others, nor does it prove itself. With the eyes of my faith I see the nonbeliever who loves his neighbor and commits himself seriously to the task of liberation and of brotherhood as "known" by God and "touched" by the grace of redemption. But I do not feel that I have any kind of power over him.

The gift of "grace" pertains to the mystery and remains within the mystery of faith.

The object is not to disturb the inner world of one who does not feel or call himself a believer. Such was already, in the Bible, the real meaning of a verse that is repeated in the Song of Songs:

> I charge you,
> daughters of Jerusalem,
> by the gazelles, by the hinds of the field,
> not to stir my love, nor rouse it,
> until it please to awake.
>
> (Sg. 2:7; 3:5; 8:4)

God himself respects the freedom and the inner consistency of the nonbeliever. And if the nonbeliever is sincere, he has the right not to believe in God; just as the believer, if he is sincere, has the right to believe.

After these explanations of the theological issues and of the need to "demythologize" the ecclesial triumphalism that affects the eschatological perspectives of the New Testament, how do I reaffirm my faith in Christ the Lord (*Kyrios*), savior of the world?

This is the place to introduce a theology of liberation and a theology of secularization, which—when properly understood—do not in any way eliminate the substance of the faith of the apostles.

> The Kingdom of God is:
> But let justice flow like water,
> and integrity like an unfailing stream.
>
> (Am. 5:24)

> With integrity and justice,
> with tenderness and love.
>
> (Ho. 2:21)

> Each morning give sound judgment,
> rescue the man who has been wronged
> from the hands of his oppressor.
>
> (Jr. 21:12)

> To break unjust fetters
> and undo the thongs of the yoke,
> to let the oppressed go free,
> and break every yoke,
> to share your bread with the hungry,
> and shelter the homeless poor,
> to clothe the man you see to be naked
> and not turn from your own kin.
>
> (Is. 58:6–7)

> Judging in favor of the orphan and exploited,
> so that earthborn man may strike fear no longer.
>
> (Ps. 10:18)

> Rescuing the poor man from the stronger,
> the needy from the man who exploits him.
>
> (Ps. 35:10)

God gives the lonely a permanent home,
makes prisoners happy by setting them free.

(Ps. 68:6)

He has pulled down princes from their thrones and exalted
the lowly.
The hungry he has filled with good things, the rich sent
empty away.

(Lk. 1:52–53)

Go and sell everything you own and give the money to the
poor.

(Mk. 10:21; Lk. 12:33)

You must love the Lord your God with all your heart. . . . You
must love your neighbor as yourself. There is no commandment
greater than these. . . . This is far more important than any
holocaust or sacrifice.

(Mk. 12:30–34)

And this hoard of yours, whose will it be then?

(Lk. 12:20; Jm. 5:3)

So always treat others as you would like them to treat you.

(Mt. 7:12)

Go and learn the meaning of the words:
"What I want is mercy, not sacrifice."

(Mt. 9:13; Ho. 6:6)

Justice, mercy, good faith, these you should have practiced.

(Mt. 23:23)

Love is never selfish, takes no pleasure in other people's sins.

(I Co. 13:5–6)

You were called to liberty. . . . Serve one another in works
of love.

(Ga. 5:1 and 13)

121

If you love your fellow men, you have carried out your obligations. . . . Love (*agape*) is the one thing that cannot hurt your neighbor.

(Rm. 13:8–10)

Pure, unspoiled religion, in the eyes of God our Father is this: coming to the help of orphans and widows when they need it, and keeping oneself uncontaminated by the world.

(Jm. 1:27)

Behave like free men, and never use your freedom as an excuse for wickedness.

(I P. 2:16)

Live for holiness.

(I P. 2:24)

Never pay back one wrong with another, or an angry word with another one. . . . If you do have to suffer for being good, you will count it a blessing. There is no need to be afraid. . . . It is better to suffer for doing right than for doing wrong.

(I P. 3:9, 14, 17)

We have passed out of death and into life,
and of this we can be sure
because we love our brothers.

(I Jn. 3:14)

Our love is not to be just words or mere talk,
but something real and active.

(I Jn. 3:18)

A man who does not love the brother that he can see
cannot love God, whom he has never seen.

(I Jn. 4:20)

Keep doing good works and sharing your resources (*koinonía*), for these
are sacrifices that please God.

(Heb. 13:16)

This view of the Kingdom of God, which is presented without any break in continuity in the whole of the Testament and in the whole of the New Testament, provides an absolute support for the theology of liberation.

To claim that evangelical liberation is "interior" or "spiritual" and not social and political, is a trick intended to protect a socially conservative form of religion and a betrayal of the Bible. The Kingdom of God applies to man in his inseparable double dimension, personal and social. There is no liberation of the heart from sin without facing up to the political problem of liberation. The reason is that the main sin from which the heart must be liberated is the sin of selfishness, of cooperation with injustice, of attachment to private wealth, of lack of generous love that works justice and drives us to work (to struggle, to commit ourselves) for liberation.

What does Christian hope, which is the inseparable content of faith in the risen Christ, seek in regard to liberation?

What Christian hope looks forward to is that the "liberation" of the heart of man (of many men, perhaps of all) will gradually take place in dialectical connection with liberation in the social, economic, and political orders; this to be the work not of apocalyptic interventions but of men themselves, of men who will never be closed to the influence of "grace" in the depth of their being, though without any necessary connection of this action of "grace" with Church structures or with identifiably religious attitude of the one who is freely benefited in the depth of his being by the gift (called "unspeakable" by St. Paul) of the Spirit of the Lord Jesus. Christian hope is prophetic. It tells us nothing of "how" it will be gradually realized in history.

Of course, history has taught us that the systems of "Christianity" are not the way of growing realization, in the course of history, of this Messianic liberation.

They are incompatible with an ethicoprophetic authenticity of the realization of visible Christianity. In consequence, their effect is rather to hold back the coming of the Kingdom of God.

The regime of "Christendom" and all kinds of politicoreligious fundamentalism are "mythological" ways of conceiving the realization of the Kingdom of God. In consequence, once they have come into existence, they have gone against the authentically eschatological current. They have been an "obstacle." And it is a sin against the Kingdom to try to preserve them or to restore them in disguised forms.

The distinction between eschatological hope and historical hope may help us to understand what eschatological hope is and what it is not (what it offers and what it does not offer the believer). The Christian whose outlook is ethicoprophetic should promote these two kinds of hope simultaneously, while keeping them distinct.

In an Introduction I wrote during the summer of 1971 for the Spanish translation of a book dealing with Christian love and class warfare, written by Giulio Girardi,[18] I tried to clarify this distinction:

Erich Fromm has gone deeply into the theme of historic hope.[19]

Authentic historic hope must be distinguished from kinds of false hope which can be deceptive forms of despair or desperation. One type of false hope is the passive hope of a solution that will occur by itself. This passive hope involves an idolatry of the future. It implies that the future, by the mere fact of being future, is going to resolve what is not being resolved or on the way to being resolved in the present. This kind of false hope ends up by becoming a disguise for despair. To leave everything in the hands of the future, when nothing is hoped of the present, is to make for oneself a pure "myth" lacking in real content and without creative power.

Another kind of false hope is the adventurism unrelated to reality (arbitrary) of irrational action. This false hope can be a disguise for desperation. One has no real hope, yet simultaneously is not ready to accept despair. He cannot accept the barren "myth" of an idolatrous future. In such circumstances, people commit themselves to action without hope, action which tends to be violent, because such is the effect of desperation.

The most pathetic form of this kind of action without hope is

---

[18] *Amor cristiano y lucha de clases* (Salamanca, 1971).
[19] Erich Fromm, *The Revolution of Hope* (New York: Haper & Row, 1968). The author used an Italian translation (Milan: Etas Kompass, 1969).

suicide of the person who is unable to face the injustice of the world and who is conscious of his own inability to change things. Such kinds of suicide sometimes provide the hope that they will help to create a greater awareness and arouse public opinion, and can consequently be beneficial. But at other times, the suicide is merely an act of rejection in a situation which is judged to have no solution and which seems intolerable.

Fromm places authentic hope, operating within history, face to face with these forms of despair or concealed desperation.

Authentic hope is active (in contrast to the passive kinds of hope) and it is capable of achievement (in contrast to unrealistic adventurism). This kind of hope presupposes a certain human and rational faith. Describing this faith, which is not to be confused with Christian religious faith, Fromm speaks to us of "knowledge of the really possible" and of the "certainty of uncertainty." His point is this: Social and historical reality cannot be reduced to a closed scientific system in which everything is already foreseen and which can only repeat the past. Social and historical reality, and also human reality in the last analysis, is essentially open. There exist possibilities of new forms moving into the future, new forms which are "out of" the present. What is at issue, in consequence, are "real" possibilities.

What Fromm calls "the certainty of uncertainty" is the certainty that something different is possible. It is not certain that a qualitative change is impossible. We are not inexorably condemned to spin around in this world of selfishness and oppression, with no hope of escape.

Fromm uses "the knowledge of the really possible" and "the certainty of uncertainty" as the foundation on which he stands his concept of "rational faith." It is "faith," because a man sets out to build for the future, committing himself to the task of constructing a world of brotherhood free from oppression, without being able to have a strictly scientific certainty that the enterprise will succeed. But it is "rational," because it is constantly supported by the search for real possibilities, careful to avoid unrealistic adventurism, while simultaneously not seeking to escape historic risk. In this way, "rational faith" is a creative power.

What relationship can we establish between Christian faith and hope and the historic hope and rational faith described by Fromm?

Christian hope and faith, if misunderstood, can lead to an attitude of passive hope in the world and in history. More precisely, the socially conservative Christian lacks genuine historic hope and lives in the passive acceptance of the world as it is, with an attitude similar to that of the passive hope of the future described by Fromm. But for this kind of Christian, the future for which he waits passively is outside the plane of history and unconnected to it. It is a "heaven" composed of lavish spectacles (to "see" God) and of "music" (to "sing" to God), which man conquers as an individual, and which is completely unrelated to what has been the historic occupation of mankind.

Is such a method of living Christian hope acceptable?

Progressive Christians of today (those who are not socially conservative, and this by reason of their understanding of the Christian faith) believe—and I am one of them—that a concept of Christian hope totally unconnected to historic hope is false, from the viewpoint of genuine Christianity.

But this can be made more specific.

Socially conservative Christians make a positive and radical dissociation of their Christian hope from historic hope. They do not possess historic hope, and their way of understanding Christian hope confirms their historic despair. As they see it, in consequence, their social conservatism and their way of understanding Christianity are joined together functionally and self-supporting, at least in practice. Lived and understood in this way, Christianity is "the opium of the people." Such a way of understanding Christianity is, in my view, false.

But does this understanding not find some support in the attitude of Jesus and of the first generation of Christians regarding earthly reality?

It is, of course, true that the eschatological system of early Christianity was formulated in the perspective of the imminent arrival of the end of the world. Without saying dogmatically and in a totally uniform way that the end of the world is close at hand, the New Testament writings are placed in the perspective (in the assumption) that time is very short.

That is obviously one of the reasons why a demand for structural change in human society is not formulated directly and immediately in the Gospel message or elsewhere in the New Testament.

But that does not mean that the eschatological system of the first Christians justifies the later marriage of two such disparate things as transhistoric eschatological hope and social conservatism.

The eschatological hope of the early Christians was not associated with an attitude of passive waiting within history, but with an attitude of active hope, even though this was formulated not on the political level of structural revolution, but on the level of an effective personal revolution which ended up by having a profound impact at the level of social structures also.

The example of Zacchaeus, as given by St. Luke (19:1–9), is typical in this regard. The conversion of Zacchaeus is a personal one, and Jesus does not demand of him an option of a revolutionary political kind in order to declare him "a son of Abraham." But his personal conversion reaches, in an extraordinarily effective way, to the roots (and to the economic and social roots) of his personal situation in society: "Look, sir, I am going to give half my property to the poor, and if I have cheated anybody I will pay him back four times the amount." If Christianity had continued in later times to formulate personal conversion in these terms, socially conservative Christianity would never have come into existence, and Christians—by virtue of their Christian faith—would have been available for the qualitative change of social structures just as soon as "the signs of the times" had signaled the historic hour of revolutionary possibility.

But even when we have got rid of the misunderstanding of a socially conservative Christianity, some other issues still need clarification.

We noted above that socially conservative Christians disassociate their Christian hope in a positive and radical way from historic hope. We have rejected this attitude. But ought we not to disassociate Christian hope from historic hope in a way I might describe as negative?

Let me explain. Christian hope does not exclude historic hope. More than that, Christian love—without which faith is dead and Christian hope lacks all basis—drives us to engage in a search for the ways of historic hope. But is it possible to say that Christian hope is positively a guarantee and a support of the attitude of one who is open to historic hope? Or must it be said that the problem of having historic hope or not having it is a distinct one and totally unrelated to Christian hope?

In other words, after we have established that Christian hope does not exclude historic hope, and that the vital union of Christianity with social conservatism distorts the nature of Christianity, can we take a further step? Can we state that Christian hope involves a radical and undeniable attitude of openness to historic hope?

It would seem at first glance that Girardi, in the final paragraphs of his already mentioned work on Christian love and revolutionary violence, excludes any vital union of Christian hope and historic hope. "At times one hears of attempts," he writes, "to establish a necessary connection between divine providence and earthly hope. How could God—it is said—allow the perpetuation of so much evil in history and thus accept the failure of the enterprise which he himself entrusted to mankind? For our part, we would answer as follows: He could continue to allow it just as he has allowed it up to now, for the same reasons which we are unable to understand. . . . It is not permissible to pass from a conservative notion of providence to a dogmatic progressivism, from a fundamentalism of the right to one of the left. Both solutions involve the same basic error, in that they expect God to provide the solution of problems he has entrusted to us, looking to God for a protection and a form of security which he does not claim to give us."

It seems to me that it is possible to go into this point more fully.

Girardi rightly rejects here an historic hope based on a "theodicy" (in the original sense of the theodicy of Leibniz), as though human reason were capable of deciding what God can permit and what he cannot. To say that God cannot permit in the future what he has permitted in the past is to fall into the already noted false form of hope which is a passive hope of the future, a mythology of the future.

Christian hope does not find its answer either in a conservative or a progressive theory of providence. It does not provide for us, on the level of history, the answer to the problem of history.

Historic hope has to be formulated and lived as an effort which helps to make real the present possibilities with regard to the fu ture. It is an active attitude with the capacity of actualizing its content. As such, it does not take its stand on any dogmatic affirmation, but on its recognition of the real possibility (existing "now" in relation to the "future"), in its certain knowledge that it is not certain that the search has to be abandoned.

From this it follows that it is an error—as Girardi properly insists—"to expect from God the solution of problems he has entrusted to us."

But if we recognize that historic hope cannot be formulated on the basis of a dogmatic faith concerning the shape of the future (whether this dogmatism fall within the category of religion or of Marxism), does this have to exclude the possibility of finding in Christian faith, based on the word of God, elements which coincide with our attitude of historic hope?

Christian eschatological hope, as it is now focused after it has overcome the illusion that the world was close to an apocalyptic end, is not the same thing as historic hope (rational faith in what is really possible), nor is it a substitute therefor. But it converges toward the attitude of historic hope. The Christian, as Christian, not only knows that "man is greater than the earth and hope stronger than death," and that "in the final analysis love never lets us down and is never wasted"; the Christian, by virtue of his Christian hope, always remains unswervingly open to historic hope: available to historic hope, fortified against the temptation to reject historic hope.

All this naturally assumes that his Christian hope is genuine and corresponds in its inmost depths to the word of God.

[At this point my Introduction goes into an explanation of Paul's testimony regarding faith in the resurrection, in Chapter 15 of the first Letter to the Corinthians, a subject already discussed. Then it continues:]

To reject historic hope is incompatible with maintaining a genuinely Christian eschatological hope.

But eschatological hope is not, in itself, historical hope, because it is formulated on the level of a supernatural (suprarational) faith and of a prophetic perspective, whereas the level of historic hope is that of a rational faith (of the "certainty of uncertainty") based on the knowledge of (on the unswerving search for) those "real" possibilities that can be discovered in the visible and verifiable web of history.

Let me sum up.

Christian hope tells us that "it makes sense" to hold on to historic hope; that historic hope is never to be abandoned. But it does not tell us the way historic hope will be realized, the shape of the future. The believer, just like the nonbeliever, and using the same tools, has to go on building the concrete projections of human hope.

Paul tells us that the victory over death (the resurrection) is the final crown of victory over all the other powers of evil. Death is the "last" of the powers to be vanquished. But we do not know if the "before" and the "after" refer strictly to the order of time and visible occurrence.

Eschatological hope places on us the risk, the responsibility, and the search as we plan and implement historic hope, which is and must be a creative potentiality of man in time, a childbirth in effort and pain.

The active and victorious lordship of Christ over history is not a datum recognizable by the senses. We can say quite properly that it is not historic. We cannot count on it when we are making the historic calculation of the possibilities of the future. Yet at the same time, this lordship—in the way the Christian affirms it by faith—is not disconnected from history.

The action of Jesus, the risen Christ, in time is not conducted by means of apocalyptic interventions. St. James does not come charging in on a white horse. God's providential care of history is not subject to measurement.

The action of Jesus is exercised in the mystery of man's heart. That is precisely where there is an opening to the possibilities of grace (*cháris*), of a gift, of the breathing of the Spirit. But in history man has to act, man all by himself.

In consequence, the genuine Christian will find himself shoulder to shoulder with all who live the historic process with creative hope. Eschatological hope will sustain him in the mystery of his personal existence, an existence open to faith and to the love of Jesus, who died and rose from the dead. That hope will sustain his mind and his heart, so that—amid the risks and uncertainties of life—he will hold ever fast to his certain knowledge that it is "humanly" possible and right to hope.

With this thought we are back once more to the subject of the theology of secularization.

That theology does not seek to deny Christianity. Dietrich Bonhöeffer, whose letters and notes from prison underlie the theological direction known as secularization, was one of the greatest Christians of all time, one of the most genuine believers in Christ among our contemporaries.

The more radical, nevertheless, among the theologians of secularization or among the Christians who share their stand seem to think that any kind of expression in a concrete form of the religious dimension, even if it does not go beyond faith in Jesus Christ and the innermost meaning of "redemption," of "grace" and of "prayer," necessarily leads to an ontological-cultist attitude and has to be gotten rid of.

These Christians believe that Christianity will be possible in the future only as a life without religion, one lived at a worldly level in the service and love of our neighbor (within a sincere commitment to justice and brotherhood), making Christian values (the Gospel) real in this way, but without any explicit form of profession of the faith.

The position of these Christians is understandable. The weight of the ontological-cultist distortion throughout the course of the history of Christianity is in fact simply overwhelming.

Nevertheless, the figure of Jesus is, for believers, adequate to free us from the temptation to make the unqualified assertion that an ethicoprophetic stand is impossible.

Our vocation as Christians, and the vocation of the Church in history, is to make real the love of the neighbor we profess, and also the ontological hope and the faith in Christ the Lord, always maintaining an ethicoprophetic stand free from every ontological-cultist ambiguity.

What will be the effect on and within history if the Church (specifically, the Roman Catholic Church, to which we belong) obstinately refuses to break out of its present ontological-cultist molds? Will God put it to one side, discarded in a blind alley, while the forward movement of "the history of salvation" and the advance of the Kingdom continue along other roads?

This we do not know.

Wherever there is progress toward justice, liberation from oppression, provision of human needs, action to correct the condition of the destitute, destruction of oppressive privileges and of class discriminations, an abhorrence of injustice and its structures, love of the neighbor and true freedom, there the Kingdom of God is on the march and we are drawing in eschatological terms closer to the *Parousia*.

Wherever these things are denied, unknown, or blocked, there the Kingdom of God is not progressing.

It seems perfectly clear to those whose religious attitude is ontological-cultist, especially if they are firm in their commitment to this line, that the Kingdom of God is at work in Rome, and that Peking is the standard bearer for those opposed to it. But there is no such evidence for the man whose life is truly guided by an ethicoprophetic religious attitude.

Who dares assert that China today is not a fermentation of the leaven of the Kingdom, and that Vatican City state is not a scabby incrustation holding back such fermentation?

St. Paul urged on the Christian community of Rome, of which the Roman Catholic Church of today is the historical continuation, an attitude of deep humility. He urged them not to think themselves superior to the other branches. He was referring to those Israelites who had hardened their hearts.

"Even if you think yourself superior to the other branches, remember that you do not support the root; it is the root that supports you. You will say, 'Those branches were cut off on purpose to let me be grafted in!' True, they were cut off, but through their own unbelief; if you still hold firm, it is only thanks to your faith. Rather than making you proud, that should make you afraid. God did not spare the natural branches, and he is not likely to spare you. Do not forget that God can be severe as well as kind: He is severe to those who fell, and he is kind to you, but only for as long as he chooses to be, otherwise you will find yourself cut off too." (Rm. 11:18–22).

The Church will maintain its life in the root of the Kingdom if it remains steadfast in faith and in goodness—in other words, if it lives the faith in an ethicoprophetic attitude. Otherwise, it will be cut off. It is possible for it to be cut off. How could that happen? Only God knows. As St. Paul adds, God is "perfectly able" to do whatever he decides.

The same call to humility and to seek in an ethicoprophetic attitude (and in nothing else) the guarantee of the Church's survival is found in those words of St. Matthew's Gospel that form the ending of the Sermon on the Mount:

"Therefore, everyone who listens to these words of mine and acts on them will be like a sensible man who built his house on rock. Rain came down, floods rose, gales blew and hurled themselves against that house, and it did not fall: It was founded on rock. But everyone who listens to these words of mine and does not act on them will be like a stupid man who built his house on sand. Rain came down, floods rose, gales blew and struck that house, and it fell; and what a fall it had!" (Mt. 7:24-27).

What is absolutely certain for me as a believer in Jesus Christ is that those who carry on that faith within an ethicoprophetic perspective, and with their faces set determinedly against ontological-cultist attitudes, are in the eschatological current of the Kingdom of God as it moves forward in history. That is where I try to keep myself, in spite of all my defects and lack of consistency.

In addition, a radical secularization (in the sense of abandoning every explicit "profession" of faith in Jesus Christ and losing every sense of "grace" and of "prayer"—at least in the field of awareness that can be conceptualized and expressed as reflex self-consciousness) does not of itself give any assurance that the man thus secularized is going to be at the service of justice and brotherhood rather than of oppression and selfishness.

That is another reason why the unconditional commitment to serve the Kingdom within an ethicoprophetic framework does not involve the option of radical secularization in the sense of a rejection of any explicit "profession" of faith in Jesus.

Besides, for those who retain this faith in the risen Lord, as I do, it is an unshakable element of eschatological hope that the true "children of the Kingdom" (those who are such for the sake of the human and mysterious Christ), even if in their historic existence they lived as atheists or as radically secularized persons, will one day meet the true Christ, and that he will say to them:

133

"Come!" That is what the parable of the last judgment, as told by St. Matthew, means.

Explicit faith, accordingly, when lived in an ethicoprophetic and coherent context, can and should be in every single case an eschatological "sign."

Above all the uncertainties of history, in open dialogue with others, with the desire to be faithful to the ethicoprophetic demands that come from the Gospel, and with the liberty He won for us, I proclaim my faith in Jesus, the Anointed (the Christ) of God, the Risen One, the Lord of time and of history.

III

Faith in Jesus Christ and Church Membership

1. What Church Membership Means

SOME OF MY YOUNG FRIENDS say to me when I explain to them what my faith means for me: "Your way of living and understanding faith in Jesus Christ seems wholly positive to us. What we don't understand is how, if this is your faith, you can continue your membership in the Catholic Church."

This is a question I must answer both for myself and for others, and I must answer it with absolute sincerity.

"To remain in the Church" is an expression that involves some ambiguity, because the word "Church" has what might be called a dialectic plurality of meanings, so that the limits of its content must necessarily remain somewhat fluid. I might put it in this way. I remain in the Church by remaining in the Roman Catholic Church, but this does not mean that the two expressions, "to stay in the Church" and "to stay in the Roman Catholic Church" are strictly and properly interchangeable.

The Church of Christ is more than the Roman Catholic Church. And the Roman Catholic Church is not always, in every respect and on all grounds, the Church of Christ.

One might perhaps say—and this would be pretty close to the

facts—that the small apostolic community of Jerusalem on the day of Pentecost was the Church of Christ. But the Roman Catholic Church of today, the Eastern Orthodox churches separated from Rome, and the Protestant churches (some more, some less, some one way, some another, as Christ will decide at the appointed time), are qualitatively very far from that original apostolic community. In consequence, all of them (in different ways) "are" and "are not" the Church of Christ. And to belong to one of them is not—unless we make the appropriate qualifications—to belong to the Church of Christ. One has to establish not only how the church to which he belongs is (visible, socially and historically identifiable), but also how (with what attitude) he belongs to it.

If we accept this starting point, a first answer to the question why I can stay in the Catholic Church might go like this: By staying in the Catholic Church, adopting an active stand (critical both of myself and of the institution) in the light of my personal, lived faith in Jesus Christ and of the spirit of the Gospel, I do what is in my power to stay in the Church of Christ. The "active stand" (which, when authentic, tends to make the hierarchy of the Roman Catholic Church nervous) is an integral element. It may not be sacrificed if that price has at times to be paid in order to remain juridically and sociologically in the Catholic Church. If a person is given the choice of either giving up this "active stand" (exercised in authentic sincerity and with liberty of conscience and based on an internal and personally lived faith) or being excluded from the Catholic Church by a legal mechanism of formal excommunication (a judgment of an ecclesiastical tribunal that condemns the accused to the status of *excommunicatus vitandus*, one not only excommunicated but to be avoided by the faithful), his choice—if he believes in Jesus Christ with a genuine faith—must be his "active stand," which is nothing more than his faith lived personally according to his conscience. The responsibility for his exclusion from the Church would fall not on him, but on those who excluded him.

136

St. Augustine seems to have had just such a case in mind in a passage worthy of attention:

Divine providence also often permits the exclusion of good men from the Christian congregation by reason of the violent opposition of men who are a prey to their lower appetites. By supporting such abuse and offense with all possible patience for the peace of the church, resisting the temptation to introduce schism or heresy, these good people show to all with what deep esteem and sincere love we should serve God. The objective of those who react in this way is either to return (to the church) when the waves have calmed, or if this proves impossible because the storm continues to rage or would only be again stirred up by their coming back, they should continue firm in their decision to see the welfare of those same people whose dealings and machinations had forced them to leave. They should consequently defend to the death the faith as preached in the Catholic church which they know, staying away from the meeting places of those who set up separate centers, and supporting the true faith by their testimony. The Father who sees in secret crowns such people in secret. Men of this caliber do not seem to be common, yet we have examples of such; indeed, they are more numerous than one might imagine.[1]

Now I shall try to explain more fully my first answer, which went like this: "By staying in the Roman Catholic Church, adopting an active stand (critical both of myself and of the institution) in the light of my personal, lived faith in Jesus Christ and of the spirit of the Gospel, I do what is in my power to stay in the Church of Christ."

Why do "I do what is in my power to stay in the Church of Christ"?

What, in its innermost essence and behind and beyond the incidents and variations on the level of history, is the Church of Christ?

To claim to be able to offer a definitive answer would be to misrepresent the question. I prefer to attempt two or three steps.

[1] *De vera religione*, 6, 11; P.L. 34, 128.

I believe in Jesus who is Christ the Lord. I have already professed and explained this faith.

But if I believe in Jesus, I am in communion with all who believe in Jesus with a genuine faith. If my faith is genuine (as I hope it is, and as my conscience tells me it is, though the last word is God's and Christ's), I am in communion with all those who believe in Jesus with a genuine faith. And this communion of faith is the Church of Christ. How would it be possible for me, a believer in Jesus, the Son of God, not to do all in my power to remain in the Church of Christ?

If I believe in Jesus and find myself in the company of another who believes in Jesus, both of us with a personal and genuine faith, a dialogue of faith will be established as a matter of course, unless the circumstances or unfavorable conditioning stand in the way. This potential dialogue of faith shared by all who possess genuine faith is also an element in our communion in faith, in our "remaining in the Church of Christ."

Let me take a step farther. Faith in Jesus is essentially ecclesial. In consequence, it is impossible to believe in Jesus, the anointed of God, without including the Church of Christ in the content of that faith. It is a church that is simultaneously historical and shrouded in mystery, existing in a tension that is inescapably dialectic.

To make of the Church an end in itself on a level that places it above history and mankind is to undermine the foundations of the Paschal faith, which was that of Peter and the Twelve, and which originated in Jerusalem at a fixed moment in history, when the risen Jesus "appears" (ófthe) to them, and they "believe" in the deep sense of "faith."

But at the same time, the historical fact of the Paschal faith of the disciples, and of the communion of faith that makes of these disciples a community, has a dimension of mystery. It cannot be reduced to terms of pure empiric analysis in the order of historic and scientific knowledge.

This dimension of mystery is also a dimension of the "demanding character" and of the "incompleteness" of the Christian Church (or the Christian churches) that exist historically: a "demanding character," because the Christian Church that exists in history should be a perfect community in the communion of a genuine (ethicoprophetic) faith; and an "incompleteness," because the community is not perfect, nor is it sufficiently genuine in its faith.

The Church in history is, in consequence, a strictly eschatological event. It is "already" but it is "not yet" the Church of Christ.

It is already, because it comes from the community of apostolic faith, in which what the Church should be was already manifest with relative fullness. But it is not yet (it does not exist, it is not realized), because of the enormous defects of genuineness in the faith of Christians in the course of history.

This eschatological tension of an historic church, which simultaneously is and is not the Church of Christ, was expressed in very clear terms by St. Augustine in his *Retractations*, which modify earlier writings in which he had much too happily assumed a pure and simple identity of the historically visible Catholic Church with the true Church of Christ: that "glorious" church "with no speck or wrinkle or anything like that, but holy and faultless," which Christ loves as his wife, as St. Paul says in the Letter to the Ephesians (5:25–27).

Here is what St. Augustine says:

I wrote seven books, *On Baptism*, against the Donatists who strive to defend themselves on the authority of the most blessed bishop and martyr Cyprian. In these, I taught that nothing is so effective as the letters and conduct of Cyprian for refuting the Donatists and completely closing their mouths so that they cannot defend their schism against the Catholic church.

But wherever in these books I have mentioned "the church not having spot or wrinkle," it should not be interpreted as if it were such now, but rather what is being prepared to be when, indeed, it will appear glorious. For now, because of certain ignorances and infirmities of its members, its condition is such that every day the entire church says: "Forgive us our debts."[2]

With this in view, if the visible Church is and is not the true Church of Christ (is and is not that Church at the same time), and if it should (at each moment) try to become such but will not achieve this objective fully until the *Parousia*, it seems to me that what Jesus asks of all who believe in him are two things: to stay in the true Church (insofar as this lies in their power) but to stay in it with an active and critical attitude (critical of oneself and of the institution) and with an unswerving Christian freedom of conscience and of expression: of "dialogue."

About the year A.D. 180, a Christian named Abercius who left his epitaph in writing says in it that in his visits to churches in very many different places, he found everywhere dialogue and the Eucharist. It is a text of hallowed associations, and it moves me deeply each time I recall it:

> My name is Abercius,
> disciple of the chaste pastor
> who feeds his flocks of sheep
> on mountains and in fields,
> and who has big eyes
> which penetrate into everything.
> He it is who taught me
> the words to be believed.
> He sent me to Rome
> to view the kingdom
> and to see the queen
> with golden robe and golden sandals.
> There I saw a people
> stamped with a wondrous mark.
> And I have seen the fields of Syria
> and all the cities, as far as Nisibe,

[2] *Retractationum*, 2, 18; P.L. 32, 637–38. English translation from *The Fathers of the Church*, Vol. 60, Sister Mary Inez Bogan, trans. (Washington, D.C.: Catholic University of America Press, 1968).

going over across the Euphrates,
and everywhere I have found ready converse,
because I had Paul. . . .
The faith has guided me in all parts
and it has given me my food,
everywhere the fish from the great fountain,
a spotless fish, such as a chaste virgin might catch
to be a banquet for her friends endlessly,
she who has the richest wine,
and offers it mixed with bread.[3]

Now I take yet another step.

This Church of Christ, which should faithfully become a concrete reality in the course of history, possesses of right a certain
authority (*exousia*), which (in some way) comes to it from Christ
in the Holy Spirit and which should be exercised by some of the
brothers inside the community. Peter, whose Paschal faith exercised a privileged and unique mediation in the birth of the very
first community of faith, "the Twelve," exercised this authority,
as did Paul, and James of Jerusalem, who was the Lord's brother
(Ga. 1:19), and the process of public recognition of those who
should exercise it was intimately joined to the pouring out of the
Spirit and with a kindling of Paschal faith in the risen Christ.

This original structure, with a ministry of presidence in the
service of the community of faith and love entrusted to identified
decision makers (*hegoúmenoi*) who were entitled to obedience
and respect (as seen in the Letter to the Hebrews, 13:17), must
have continued beyond the first generation of Christians, and
joined (in one way or another) to the original experience. There
must be some kind of "apostolic succession."

All this, moreover, comes from Christ himself, not in the sense
that Jesus, the Christ of God, performed any judicial act of institution either during his life on earth or (even less) after his resurrection, but because it is intrinsically joined to the original ex-

[3] M. J. Rouët de Journel, *Enchiridion Patristicum*, No. 187.

perience of the ecclesial community of faith, and this Paschal faith and this community of faith come from Jesus. In addition, there is no reason to doubt that Jesus, during his life, spoke and acted regarding "the Twelve," and particularly in regard to Peter, in a way that established and conditioned the function Peter and the Twelve exercised in the first community of faith.

It can be said in this sense that Jesus Christ conferred on the Church (as it exists historically) authority (*exousía*) in the Holy Spirit, and even that he has entrusted the exercise of this authority to certain individuals inside the community.

If I believe, as I do, that Jesus is the Lord, and thus come to be a sharer in the Paschal faith of the apostles, I cannot do less than accept as part of that faith the essential elements in the ecclesial happening, which includes the essential aspects of a certain structure of power exercised by certain individuals in the name of Christ, a power to which I remain open and available. This attitude pertains to my life of faith.

But the meaning of this authority or power, which exists (or should exist) in the Church, must not be distorted or exaggerated.

We are not dealing with a political or quasipolitical "power" that can be backed up with force or adopt authoritarian methods. All that is envisaged in the two Letters of Paul to the Corinthians that have come down to us is in the direction of a dialectic of authority and dialogue (which includes elements of persuasion and appeal at the same time as it affirms the apostolic authority). If this paradoxical quality of authority in the Church is not understood, neither will it be possible to understand Paul's paradoxical statement: "Once you have given your complete obedience, we are prepared to punish any disobedience" (II Co. 10:6).

The paradoxical character of ecclesial power, which is *the very opposite* of human power of a political nature, is expressed in a statement recorded by the three synoptic evangelists. The version given in St. Matthew's Gospel (which, elsewhere, stresses more than any of the others the power entrusted to the Church) is as follows: "You know that among the pagans the rulers lord it over them, and their great men make their authority felt. [In Luke's version, there is an ironic overtone: "Those who have authority over them are given the title Benefactor." (Lk. 22:25).] This is not to happen among you. No; anyone who wants to be great among you must be your servant, and anyone who wants to be first among you must be your slave [in Luke's version—22:26—"the leader as if he were the one who serves"], just as the Son of Man came not to be served but to serve, and to give his life as a ransom for many." (Mt. 20:25-28).

There exists a tendency to conceive of ecclesial authority as an absolute quasipolitical power, though with a spiritual purpose and to be exercised with moderation and justice, the judgment on this point, however, belonging exclusively to the conscience of the "prince," as in the case of "enlightened despotism." I regard this tendency as a serious deviation, a contradiction of the Gospel and of the outlook of the prophets. We read in St. Matthew's Gospel: "You, however, must not allow yourself to be called Rabbi, since you have only one Master, and you are all brothers. You must call no one on earth your father, since you have only one Father, and he is in heaven. Nor must you allow yourselves to be called teachers, for you have only one Teacher, the Christ. The greatest among you must be your servant." (Mt. 23:8-11).

Ezekiel, in a Messianic context in Chapter 34, asserts that the shepherds of Israel are feeding themselves, not their flocks, and that in consequence the Lord Yahweh is proclaiming that there will be no more shepherds, because he himself will feed his flock. And he will judge between those sheep guilty of oppression and those that are poor and oppressed. And he will send one shepherd and one alone, the Christ, the son of David, and there will not be any shepherd other than him: "I mean to raise up one shepherd, my servant David, and to put him in charge of them and he will pasture them; he will pasture them and be their shepherd." (Ezk. 34:23).

The Church needs a function of pastoral service, but much more in a brotherly sense than in a fatherly one, and never authoritarian. Pope Clement I had some notable things to say in this regard in his Letter to the Corinthians, when he was acting as mediator in a conflict between the people and their bishop:

"This is what I think. Those who were appointed by the ones already mentioned (our apostles) or later by other worthy men with the consent of the entire church, and who have exercised their ministry in relation to the flock of Christ with sensitive humility, in an atmosphere of peaceableness and without concern for their own interests, as is confirmed by the testimony of all over a long period of time, we do not think it just that such men should be removed from their ministry."[4]

The way in which the structures of ecclesiastical "power" of today's Catholic Church function is much too far removed from its origins, and in contradiction to them to an excessive extent.

Without denying the primacy of Peter, it must be said that this primacy (like all the authority of the bishops) is inescapably of a relative nature, because of the exclusivity of the primacy of Christ, and because of the community character of the unity of the whole Church, which can exist only as a brotherhood.

There is a passage of St. Augustine that explores these concepts, a passage that first impressed itself on me many years ago:

(As Christ acted when he taught them to say, "Forgive us our debts"), so does the church act in blessed hope through this troublous life; and this church, symbolized in its generality, was personified in the Apostle Peter, on account of the primacy of his apostleship. (*Ecclesiae . . . gerebat figurata generalitate personam.*) For, as regards his proper personality, he was by nature one man (*unus homo erat*), by grace one Christian (*unus christianus*), by still more abounding grace one, and yet also, the first apostle; but when it was said to him, "I will give unto thee the keys of the kingdom of heaven, and whatsoever thou shalt bind on earth, shall be bound in heaven; and whatsoever thou shalt

---

[4] Clement, *Epistola I ad Corinthios*, 44, 3.

loose on earth, shall be loosed in heaven," he represented the universal church, which in this world is shaken by divers temptations, that come upon it like torrents of rain, floods and tempests, and falleth not because it is founded upon a rock (*petra*), from which Peter received his name. For *petra* (rock) is not derived from Peter, but Peter from *petra*; just as Christ is not called so from the Christian, but the Christian from Christ. For on this very account the Lord said, "On this rock will I build my church," because Peter had said, "Thou are the Christ, the Son of the living God." On this rock, therefore, he said, which thou hast confessed, I will build my church. For the rock (*petra*) was Christ; and on this foundation was Peter himself also built. For other foundation can no man lay than that is laid, which is Christ Jesus. The church therefore, which is founded in Christ, received from him the keys of the kingdom of heaven in the person of Peter, that is to say, the power of binding and loosing sins. For what the church is essentially in Christ, such representatively is Peter in the rock (*petra*); and in this representation Christ is to be understood as the rock, Peter as the church."[5]

St. Augustine does not deny the primacy of Peter in this passage, but rather affirms it.

He does, however, deliver a hard blow to the temptation to "mythologize" the primacy, to understand it as something located above (and consequently outside) the Church as a whole, instead of as a limited function of a universal church that should be strictly a community of dialogue and participation, in the communion of faith and of the eucharist, of hearts and goods. (But where today can we find this true Church of Christ?)

Authentic ecclesial life is a dialectic of liberty (of conscience, of faith, of search) and of obedience to ministers who guide the community and watch over the faithful.

The pole of "liberty," without suppressing the pole of obedience and docility, is heavily stressed. Polycrates of Ephesus made a beautiful comment on this point in a letter to Pope Victor I,

[5] *In Ioannis Evangelium*, 124, 5; P.L. 35, 1973-74. English translation from *Nicene and Post-Nicene Fathers*, Philip Schaff, ed., Vol. VII (Grand Rapids, Mich.: William B. Eerdmans, 1956), p. 450.

toward the end of the second century, concerning the date of the celebration of Easter: "I, therefore, my brother, being seventy-five years old in the Lord, having consulted with my brothers in all parts, and having studied the whole of Sacred Scripture, am not disturbed by threats. For those who were greater than I passed on the saying, 'We must obey God rather than men.' "[6]

The synthesis is to be found in love, which ensures that liberty does not degenerate into license and renders us all in love servants of the others (Ga. 5:1 and 13).

Early in 1971, the Christian community of Isolotto* (Florence, Italy) sent me a questionnaire, which they sent at the same time to other theologians. It raised the following issues:

We wish to set out the questions to which we request answers from the theologians, but without tying them down. *What do you think:*

1. Of the perception reached by so many Christian communities which have reached the conclusion that the ecclesiastical institution is a power structure converting the liturgical and sacramental apparatus in fact into an obstacle on the road of faith and consequently an obstacle to the liberation of men?

2. Of the decision made by such communities to remain as long as they can within the institution, in order so to recover the evangelical values that they will be able to place them at the service of the way of liberation of the oppressed, and also in order to remain united to all that part of mankind which is still to be found within the institution itself?

3. Of the repression, more or less open of these communities by the hierarchy?

4. Of the "liberty" with which these communities regard themselves as the "subject" of the celebration of the eucharist, and in consequence having the right either to dispense with it, or to celebrate it under the direct evangelical impulse of the Spirit which "blows where it will"?

[6] Eusebius de Cesarea, *Historia Ecclesiastica*, 5, 24; P.G. 20, 496–97.

* *Editor's Note:* Cardinal Ermenegildo Florit of Florence, Italy, was widely criticized for dismissing, in 1968, the pastor of the community of Isolotto who had publicly criticized the church as allied to the rich. Isolotto's 10,000 people supported the pastor, and the community has since lived in acute tension with the church structures.

5. Of a church which tolerates the interference of the civil power in matters related to internal differences of opinion within the Christian community?

On April 8 of the same year I answered as follows:

1. I believe it is true that the ecclesiastical institution functions not infrequently as a power structure, supported by other temporal power structures which are often unjust and oppressive, and in alliance with them. But I do not think that the ecclesiastical structure functions always and exclusively as a power structure.

2. A Christian community (a parish community, a spontaneous group, etc.) can and should try to recover the evangelical values in a way that will ensure that they are true (authentic) in the execution of programs for the liberation of the oppressed. The desire of these communities to do everything possible to stay in the institution and to remain united to all that part of mankind which is still to be found within the institution should not, in my opinion, reflect a merely tactical attitude. By this I mean that the institution should not be regarded as a purely historical thing, which each of us is free to take or leave as seems best to him, but which it is prudent not to leave for the reason that it can be politically helpful in the work of freeing the oppressed. The desire to remain in the institution should reflect the desire to retain communion with those who believe in Christ and in the evangelical values, and who themselves remain in the institution. It should simultaneously reflect the conviction that the institution, in its innermost core, comes in some way from Christ himself. I believe that this firm belief arises out of the content of the Christian faith. The institution is, however, by its very nature, a service of the Gospel, and we have to do all we can to ensure that it is such in fact.

3. The more or less open repression by the hierarchy of the Christian communities which criticize the ecclesiastical institution (to the extent that it is a "power structure") and seek to recover the evangelical values by incorporating them into the historic process of the liberation of the oppressed, is frequently unjust and opposed to "the obedience of the faith." This, in my view, has happened in the case of Isolotto.

4. That a community unjustly dealt with by its bishop should regard itself as the "subject" of the celebration of the eucharist, enjoying the right either to dispense with its celebration, or to

celebrate it under an evangelical impulse dictated directly by the Spirit and independently of the bishop's wishes, in a situation of extreme conflict caused by the bishop's abuse of his powers and the defective condition of the institution, does not seem to me deserving of condemnation, and it may be necessary to maintain the faith of this community, a value which is higher than the duty of disciplinary obedience to the institution. But the tendency of the "breath" of the Spirit is toward the unity of the communities in the Church and toward the creation of harmony between the spiritual impulse and the exercise of the authority which Jesus Christ has given his Church in the Holy Spirit to enable it to fulfill its task of continuing in the world the mission of Christ. Jesus Christ has entrusted the exercise of this authority within the Church to certain individuals. It is an authority which is not to be thought of as unconditional or arbitrary, because it is a service to the Church. The whole of the Church should affirm continuously its responsibility for the continuance of the original mission of the apostles.

5. It seems to me that a church which tolerates the interference of the civil authorities as regards the internal dimensions of the Christian community, betrays (except in extreme cases of riot and violence with bloodshed, or similar situations) the spirit of the faith and of the ecclesial communion (see I Co. 6:1).

These documents were published in a book dealing with the Isolotto conflict later in the same year.[7]

And now I have been able to develop my thought (my reflections on my faith) more fully in this book.

2. Catholicism, Ecumenism, and Eschatological Ecclesial Tension

NOT VERY LONG AGO, a sweet girl, a young medical doctor, confided to me—with considerable anguish—that she did not see clearly why she was a Catholic rather than a member of some other Christian denomination.

I told her that it seemed to me that nobody sees this clearly,

[7] *Isolotto sotto proceso* (Bari: Laterza, 1971), pp. 228–29 and 241–43.

and that those who think they do are the victims of an illusion based on ignorance or bias.

But the question is there. Why am I a member of the Roman Catholic Church rather than one of the other Christian churches that exist historically? It is a question I must answer for myself and for others with the total sincerity demanded in a genuine life of faith.

The conclusions derivable for the sciences of history and criticism do not seem to me adequate for answering the question. I sincerely believe that it is not possible to prove with absolute certainty, at the level of historical science, that Jesus Christ wishes all Christians to belong to the Roman Catholic Church as it exists today, giving up their membership in every other Christian church for that purpose. I have to smile at the very thought of such a claim.

If this is so, we are dealing rather with a choice related to the level of faith. But in what sense and to what extent is that the case?

I shall try to answer to myself, analyzing what seems to me to be my faith situation.

I was baptized in the Catholic Church before the end of my first month outside my mother's womb.

I came to the faith in the Catholic Church.

The dynamism of my faith leads me to remain in the Catholic Church with an "active attitude" (critical both of myself and of the Church), with an ecumenical spirit (vis-à-vis the other Christian churches), and with eschatological tension (hope), seeking to achieve through remaining historically in the Catholic Church a dynamic association (growing and becoming constantly fuller) with the Church of Christ, and a continuous building up of this Church of Christ, which will achieve its fullness only in the *Parousia*.

The dynamism of my faith does not lead me to change my church, but only to seek within the Catholic Church this ever fuller association with and progressive building up of the Church of Christ.

For me that is enough.

The dynamism of my faith does not lead me to deny that this association with the Church of Christ and this progressive building up of that church can be sought in other historically existing Christian churches.

I believe that the loyalty of my adhesion to the Roman Catholic Church does not demand in any way that I should deny that it is possible to seek and to realize (dynamically and eschatologically) in other Christian churches this association with the Church of Christ.

Why should it make such a demand of me?

What is truly needed is that all the churches and all the members of the churches should be humble and should base their Christianity, their devotion to their church, and their ecumenism exclusively on "the faith that makes its power felt through love" (Ga. 5:6).

Is it possible that the dynamism of their faith in Jesus Christ (the breathing of the Spirit) might in some circumstances bring Christians who belong to churches other than the Roman Catholic Church to "change" their church affiliation and join the Roman Catholic Church?

That is not a question I have to answer.

Neither do I have to decide whether or not it is impossible for a Catholic to be brought by the dynamism of his faith to "change" to another church.

Are we in a position to trace the roads the Spirit must take?

What must be done in every case is respect the conscientious choice a Christian feels bound to make. We must leave the responsibility to them and the judgment to God. As St. Paul says in the Letter to the Romans (14:4): "It is not for you to condemn someone else's servant; whether he stands or falls it is his own master's business; he will stand, you may be sure, because the Lord has power to make him stand."

To those who may regard my ecclesial stand as excessively "relativist," I would answer that it is precisely my faith in Jesus Christ that compels me to relativize the Church as it exists in history. It is the ontological-cultist concept that tends to absolutize the visible structures of the Church.

Some relativization of the Christian churches in the form in which they have developed historically follows inescapably not only from ecumenism that is pursued in a spirit of sincerity, but above all from the dimension of mystery in the Church of Christ (incapable of being "locked" into sociological and juridical categories) and from the resultant eschatological tension to which are subjected all the Christian communities groping their way through history under a perpetual pressure to be converted.

3. *To Believe in Jesus Christ Alone*

MY MEMBERSHIP in the Catholic Church, consciously and freely maintained by me, brings with it the duty to accept the truths defined *ex cathedra* as pertaining to the body of truths of faith (*depositum fidei*) by the ecumenical councils or by the Popes.

This does not mean that I accept a "monolithic" understanding of the Church's solemn magisterium and of its infallibility.

The question of interpretation arises with regard to the texts of the solemn magisterium at least as much as with regard to Sacred Scripture.

In addition, historical issues come into play when we seek to determine whether in fact we are dealing with a definition *ex cathedra*.

I believe that in good theology and in genuine faith (free of "mythologies") the infallibility of solemn definitions is simply this: The defined proposition can (and should) be understood in a sense that is not purely and simply false; and this "sense" (at least in broad terms) was not entirely absent from the minds of those who proclaimed the definition.

Obviously, definitions can have a much more perfect truth content than this "minimum." But the dogma of infallibility does not *a priori* guarantee for us more than that "minimum."

On the other hand, as regards the ordinary magisterium of the Popes, a strict "demythologization" is called for. This magisterium has no elements of infallibility. It can be mistaken, and it has in fact been mistaken. In issues affecting the Bible it has been outrageously mistaken for decades at a stretch. I choose this as the most indisputable example, one that nobody would today attempt to deny.

In reaching their decisions in the exercise of the ordinary magisterium, all the Popes have to count on, on the level of supernatural assistance, is the grace of state. But the effectiveness of this so-called grace of state is conditional.

This is not to say that the Popes should not exercise an ordinary magisterium, or that the faithful do not have a duty to listen with due respect to this magisterium, which possesses its own moral authority. But here, in the final analysis, the climate is one of dialogue and liberty.

Within the framework of this position of sincere and unambiguous acceptance of dogmatic "definitions" of the Catholic Church, I have for a number of years been faced with a critical difficulty.

My problem has been that in traditional theology, at least as I know it, such definitions have to be given an assent "of faith."

Now, the truths defined by the Church about itself, its properties and its prerogatives (especially papal primacy and infallibility) are based on a kind of "extrapolation" of certain passages in the New Testament, especially in St. Matthew's Gospel. And it is not fully established historically that these passages give us the actual words Jesus spoke. We cannot exclude the possibility that they contain an interpretation given by the first generation of Christians, in the light of the Paschal faith and the experience of the infant Church.

It is commonly recognized that the texts of Matthew (16:18–19;

18:18) and of John (20:23; 21:15–17) have elements of extrapolation, because these texts are regarded as confirming the Catholic viewpoint *saltem in luce traditionis* (at least in the light of tradition).

This would mean that the Church would be asking us to believe in her right to certain prerogatives, which are themselves the reason we should accept her word. And these prerogatives may perhaps not have been proclaimed by Jesus, but are set out as a self-affirmation of the ecclesial conscience.

Is not all of this much too paradoxical?

Is it not all far too human to allow us to claim that the "yes" of "faith" in the strict sense is here at issue?

I did not want either to deny my loyal membership in the Catholic Church or to play with the faith, which is a free gift we do not own, and which we should always carry forward with immense sincerity and respect.

During a spiritual retreat about four years ago, I tried to clarify my position, seeking a solution in a kind of "joyous irony of the faith," which I think is not alien to good theology.

As a result of my prayers and meditations, I wrote the following note:

Our knowledge of the mystery of the Church (in which we believe, as pertaining to the "mystery" of Christ the only Lord "on whom"—*in quem*—we believe) must include the following fact: The way in which the Church actually exists in history does not correspond to the predominant (if not exclusive) focus in which the Church is viewed in the New Testament writings. This focus is that of a special eschatology, in which the Church would continue in a perfectly straight line—without a deviation—the triumph of Easter and the pouring out of Pentecost, all the way to the *Parousia*. This is a "focus" that colors the New Testament revelation, without itself being a datum of revelation. The revealed datum should be accepted with an awareness of its coloration by a "focus" that is not completely true to the later reality of history (of the "history of salvation").

What the Roman Catholic Church says about itself with the intention of defining *ex cathedra* the content of revelation (specifically, concerning its *powers* and its infallibility) is affirmed in faith by those who believe in Christ within the Catholic Church.

Faith is "obedience"—a living union—to Jesus our Lord, to his Good News, to his teaching, his truth, his call (Rm. 1:5; 16:26; 15:8; Ac. 6:7; II Co. 10:5; Heb. 5:9; Rm. 10:16; II Th. 1:8; Rm. 6:16–17; 16:17–19. I P. 1:22; Heb. 11:8). The living "truth" of the faith is rooted in love (Ep. 4:15). Faith is essentially "freedom" in Christ (Ga. 5:13; II Co. 3:17). The acceptance by the believer of the teaching of the Church always occurs through faith "on Christ." It follows that the obedience of faith to the rule of teaching regarding the institution and *powers* (?) of the Church can and should always be saturated with a deep ecclesial humility in the presence of Christ and of the Father (opposed to every form of triumphalism) and with a living awareness of the "mystery" that the Church is (an awareness opposed to every tendency calculated to simplify—mythologize) what the word of God has told us about the Church.

In this attitude of ecclesial humility and in this awareness of the mystery, everything we believe about the Church is believed in virtue of faith "on Christ," which brings us to the visible (institutionalized) Church in history, but making us pass without ceasing (in a very concrete and living way) beyond the visible reality of the Church, which in the light of faith always seems mysteriously ambiguous (true and false at the same time, because it has risen with Christ and simultaneously is sinful). Thus, in the faith of the believer, as regards the powers of the Church defined *ex cathedra* by virtue of its powers, there is room for a kind of spiritual—theological—"humor" lived in love. Not only does such "humor" not exclude the authenticity of the faith, but it seems to answer its deepest needs.

In our meditation on the Church there is a central question that we should not try to avoid. To what extent is the Church here on earth, and has it been in the course of history, a house built on sand through failure to carry the words of Jesus into effect? (Mt. 7:24–27).

The Song of Songs can illuminate (within the mystery) the drama of Christ and his Church in the course of history (Sg. 2:8–9 and 15–17; 3:5; 5:2–8; 6:2–3; 8:1–2 and 4–7). The presence of the Word of God in the history of salvation (incomprehensively mysterious: See Pr. 8:22 and 27–31) is "already" made real with mysterious fullness in the redeeming victory of the resurrection, by means of which the "people of God" were brought into being (Col. 1:15–17). But the deep reality of this victory "already" won transcends by far the reality of the Church we see in history, as long as the *Parousia*—which is the object of our hope (Rm. 8:24)—has "not yet" arrived.

Our faith never has its radical foundation in the Church but in Christ, who is greater than the Church, and who is the one name given us in the world by which we can be saved (Ac. 4:12).

The above comment mentions the distinction between "believing" a person and "believing on" a person. Jesus Christ is the only one "on" whom we believe. We can believe an apostle, but we cannot believe "on" him.

The distinction comes from St. Augustine, who formulated it in a profound passage in his commentary on St. John's Gospel:

"This is the work of God, that you believe on him whom he has sent." *That you believe on him;* not, that you believe him. But if you believe *on* him, you believe him; yet he that believes him does not necessarily believe on him. For even the devils believed him, but they did not believe on him. Again, moreover, of his apostles we can say, we believe Paul; but not, we believe on Paul: we believe Peter; but not, we believe on Peter. For, "to him that believeth on him that justifieth the ungodly, his faith is counted unto him for righteousness" (Rm. 4:5). What then is "to believe on him"? By believing to love him, by believing to esteem highly, by believing to go into him and to be incorporated in his members. It is faith itself then that God exacts from us: And he finds not that which he exacts, unless he has bestowed what he may find. What faith, but that which the apostle has most amply defined in another place, saying, "Neither circumcision availeth anything, nor uncircumcision, but faith that worketh by love." (Ga. 5:6)?[8]

The "yes" of faith is directed to the person of Jesus and to what Jesus is (the Christ of God, the redeemer of mankind, the Lord of history, the Son of God).

The very words of Christ, to the extent that we can reach them, also receive the "yes" of faith because they are the immediate manifestation of the person of Jesus.

[8] *In Ioannis Evangelium,* 29, 6; P.L. 35, 1631. English translation from *Nicene and Post-Nicene Fathers,* op. cit., p. 185.

A dialectic between the attitude of faith and critical, historical science here comes into play. It is one that can never reach an absolute resolution. The more certain we can be that specific words in the Gospels are the very words spoken by Jesus, the more a strict "yes" of faith will be centered on them.

But the words of Scripture in general, especially those of the New Testament, at least as a whole, receive the "yes" of my faith, because they constitute a privileged mediation of the Paschal faith. And the faith of each of us is a participation in the Paschal faith of the apostles and disciples.

The "yes" of faith to the Scriptures is, nevertheless, not comparable to the "yes" of faith to the person of Jesus. Scripture is an essential mediation, but faith "on" Jesus goes beyond mediation to reach Jesus himself, the Christ, in an interior revelation.

As St. Augustine says, we believe Peter and Paul, but we do not believe on them, because we believe only "on" Jesus.

Finally, is there a response of a "yes" of faith in the strict sense from my side to the *ex cathedra* teachings of the ecumenical councils and of the Popes, when they do not limit themselves to repeating the words of Scripture, but make extensive interpretations or resolve difficult problems of interpretation?

In the notes I made four years ago, I answered that there was here a question of a "yes" of faith, but qualified by a shade of "humor."

It may well be that this interpretation is theologically the most finely honed and even the most profound.

But perhaps it is simpler (and possibly more sincere) to say that it is a "yes" tied to my faith in Jesus Christ and to the inclusion of the "mystery" of the Church in the content of my faith in Jesus Christ, a mystery whose outlines are hazy because it is of its nature dialectic: history and eschatology, yes and no, visible and invisible. I have already explained at length what I mean by these opposites.

But this "yes" to the *ex cathedra* teachings of the Church's magisterium is perhaps not a "yes" of faith in the strict sense for me, not even on the level on which our "yes" to the Gospels is a "yes" of faith.

In any case, it is not my self-consciousness that can give the final word regarding the reality of my faith. That will come from Jesus on the mysterious day we meet.

IV

Celibacy for the Kingdom of God and Sex

I AM IN MY SIXTY-FIRST YEAR and I have never been involved in an amorous escapade.

I say this without any boasting whatever, because it may well be the fact is due in part to my dumbness.

But I also say it simply and joyfully, without the slightest undercurrent of frustration or resentment.

I believe I have achieved during my life a level of communication, of understanding, and of friendship with many men and women which, in addition to giving a fundamentally radiant meaning to my life, has gradually shaped in me a personality reasonably free (at least as I see it) from unresolved tensions, frustration complexes, and pathological inhibitions.

I will complete my "dossier" by saying that, if I am not mistaken, I am definitely heterosexual. And by no manner of means a misogynist.

I wanted to put these facts—which are in themselves of no interest—on the record so as to facilitate an evaluation (more or less, according to different points of view) of the reflections and experiences I am about to present.

I made a vow of chastity (a choice of celibacy for the sake of the Kingdom of God) in private form when I was in my twentieth year, and renewed it publicly a year later, on August 16, 1932. On July 15, 1943, I was ordained a priest of the Latin rite, with an obligation of celibacy, and on February 2, 1948, I repeated the religious vow of chastity in a form that canon law of the Church regards as "solemn."

The first thing I want to say is that I am not a "hero" of chastity.

Next I want to say that, at least as a general rule, a "heroism" of chastity does not seem to me to make much sense. A person either has a certain charismatic grace in sufficient measure to make himself voluntarily a celibate for the Kingdom of God, or he is trying to deal with this celibacy on the basis of ascetic effort and self-control without an adequate charismatic "gift." In the former case, even though the celibacy for the Kingdom of God calls for some conquest of self and a level of sacrifice, just like everything that is truly good, enjoyable, and human in this life, it is not unduly difficult, and it is basically positive and joyous. In the latter case, celibacy for the Kingdom of God become a "lunatic factory," and I advise all who find themselves in this trap to free themselves from it as soon as they can, because I do not regard such "heroic" celibacy as the genuine celibacy for the Kingdom of God, which is an eschatological sign of charismatic character.

And here we come to a first theme for reflection.

I believe that the Catholic Church, in its official statements and in its predominant and traditional mentality, has for many centuries been approaching the theme of celibacy for the Kingdom of God in a mistaken way. My statement is serious, but the fact I state is far more serious. And I am convinced that the fact is real, because the statement appears to me to be true. For that reason, I regard it as my duty to speak with absolute sincerity. Of course, no *ex cathedra* definition of the ecclesiastical magisterium is at issue here. But very many scandals and sufferings rooted in the mistaken way the Church has faced the problem are at issue. That is enough reason for a Christian to talk about the matter, according to his loyal knowledge and understanding, with total clarity and sincerity.

The basic error has been to regard marriage as a state of "imperfection" and celibacy as a state of "perfection."

During the Second Vatican Council, many theologians dedicated to Church renewal fought to overcome that error, and they succeeded in having the dogmatic Constitution on the Church (*Lumen Gentium*) assert clearly that "all the faithful, of every state and condition, are called to the fullness of the Christian life and to the perfection of love" (No. 40). But the more traditional theologians, especially members of religious orders (though with some exceptions), unleashed a counteroffensive. Its object was to introduce an addition stating (after admitting in clear words that all states of Christian life are states of "perfection" for those who are faithful to the Gospel in their lives, and that none is such if this lived fidelity to the Gospel is absent) that marriage is indeed a "state of perfection" but "less perfect" in comparison with celibacy for the Kingdom of God. And they were successful in introducing into the conciliar text a phrase that in their view said that the married state is "less perfect," but that in fact does not necessarily bear that meaning. The phrase (No. 42) is as follows: "The holiness of the Church is also fostered in a special way by the observance of the manifold counsels proposed in the Gospel by our Lord to his disciples." Outstanding among them is that precious gift of divine grace which the Father gives to some men (cf. Mt. 19:11; I Co. 7:7) so that by virginity, or celibacy they can more easily devote their entire selves to God alone with undivided heart (cf. I Co. 7:32–34). This statement is based on St. Paul, a man who would seem to have understood better the positive aspects of celibacy for the Kingdom of God undertaken with a special charismatic grace, than the positive aspects of marriage lived in human and Christian fullness. St. Paul's text (and also Canon 10 of the Council of Trent concerning marriage) can be interpreted to mean that marriage lived in a Christian manner and celibacy for the Kingdom of God are two qualitatively distinct "charisms." There is truly a "charism" of celibacy for the Kingdom of God (as there is a "charism" of marriage lived in a Christian manner), and this charism of celibacy is an excellent gift, which should not be underestimated. The specific content of this celibacy contains positive and characteristic values that are not found in marriage. From this viewpoint, it is possible to say (with some bias) that celibacy is more suitable or "better" than marriage. This does not mean that there may not be other aspects under which marriage lived in a Christian manner may not be "better" than celibacy (that is to say, contain positive and excellent values not found in celibacy).

In actual fact, this whole question is somewhat academic, because what is certain is that both marriage lived in a Christian manner and celibacy for the Kingdom of God are excellent and cannot be engaged in without a "charism." What is best for each person is what corresponds to his own "charism."

What was bad about all this was that serious results followed from regarding celibacy as a state of perfection and marriage as a state of imperfection.

It is these consequences that gave its seriousness to the mistaken way in which the Church has seen the question of marriage and celibacy.

The reason is that, if we start from the idea that celibacy is synonymous with perfection and marriage synonymous with imperfection, the call to perfection (to a generous acceptance of the Gospel) is identified with the call to celibacy for the Kingdom of God. Once this is done, it is inevitable that people who lack the needed "charism" but feel a general call to perfection will be steered into the way of celibacy.

It is possible that the majority of those professing celibacy for the sake of the Kingdom of God in the Catholic Church have been pushed into that channel without having the "charism." It seems to me absolutely certain that at least many are in this state.

To speak for myself, I entered the religious novitiate in my nineteenth year with a very sincere—and reasonably free—impulse to seek a more generous acceptance of the Gospel, but without distinguishing this general call to perfection from the "charism" of celibacy. All my subsequent experience makes me believe I had this charism in an adequate degree. But I might not have had it. With the conditionings of its teaching (in the way in which this was understood) and of its techniques of applying its teaching in practice, the Church set me on a way that might have proved a fatal snare.

I am convinced that maintaining obligatory celibacy for the priesthood of the Latin rite creates a conditioning that—irrespective of intention—causes many to choose a life of celibacy without the appropriate charism.

And what is the sense of making celibacy compulsory for priests, if the charism of marriage lived in a Christian manner and the charism of celibacy undertaken for the sake of the Kingdom of God are not one "better" and one "worse," but rather both excellent, qualitatively distinct, within an "economy" of charisms that corresponds to a structure of pluralism and complementariness?

What happens is that people continue to think, or at least that many (among those in charge of the ecclesial community) retain in their subconscious the idea, that sex is in itself a thing that is always "bad," even though it achieves in marriage some level of acceptability, basically because of the need for sex in order to increase the human race.

This is an unfortunate error, and it has had a horrible impact within the Church, century after century. Even today it has not been fully eliminated.

Not only is it an unfortunate error, it is also something to drive people out of their minds. The sexual dimension is something that is in the innermost being of humans from the time they are in their mother's womb up to their death. If this is essentially "evil," man either gives himself over to evil or he loses his mind in his efforts to deny what is a dimension of his very being.

But if sex is so natural and so primary, why should it be evil? If God has created sex as something intimately constitutive of man's being (and we believe this to be so, with a clear realization of the unfathomably mysterious character of that act of "creation"), how could it be bad in itself? Or why should it have to be submitted, in order to be good, to such conditionings that human beings would be compelled to spend the greater part of their existence struggling desperately to suppress in themselves a sexual dimension that belongs during their entire existence on earth to their inner structure?

This takes me to the problem of sexual morality as taught officially in the Church.

That moral teaching, both in itself and in the way it is concretely understood and practiced, leads to indescribable sufferings from scruples, to crazy inhibitions, and to insupportable tensions.

I have seen others subjected to such sufferings, and I was myself also subjected to them until I succeeded in freeing myself from some of the formulations and aspects of the traditional theology, substituting for them other evaluations based entirely on Christian teaching and the word of God, and also to be found in the traditional teaching, although smothered there by the weight of rules conditioned by the false idea that sex outside marriage and in addition directed in some way to procreation, is evil throughout the entire range of its manifestations unless one is contradicting by an act of the will even the most simple and spontaneous reactions of a sexual nature that arise in a person.

I may seem to exaggerate, and it may be that a traditional moralist, who is precise and a clear thinker, would make further distinctions. But at the concrete and existential level, the rules of sexual morality that we lived were very much what I have just described.

I have, for many years now, followed with a tranquil conscience a sexual morality of "principles" (demanding and truly illuminating principles), and I have been freed from the grasp of certain rigid propositions that are not, in my view, well founded, and that lead to existentially absurd situations and to intolerable casuistry.

I will go farther. My personal experience has been that the substitution of a morality of "principles" for the morality of "propositions" did not lead to a loose way of living or the depravity that was feared. I believe I have lived with moral sense the sexual dimension of my existence, but without any hopeless struggle to deny sex and "to say that I am unwilling" when faced with the most basic vital manifestation of the area of sex drives. I do not pay tribute to any sexual "puritanism," but I believe I live morally as far as sex is concerned, this in a way appropriate to one who has chosen to live a celibate life for the sake of the Kingdom of God.

I have been working for seven or eight years on the problem of moving from a morality of "propositions" to one of "principles." I think that I have now clarified the issue fairly well, and I shall synthesize the results I have reached.

Moral law should not be conceived as a code of "propositions" comparable to the articles of a code of positive law. It is not *codifiable* in this manner. The failure to keep this fact sufficiently in account is one of the roots of the present crisis of morality.

The tendency to reduce morality to a kind of codification of "propositions" from moral theology texts and of "answers" from the Apostolic Penitentiary has existed among Catholics. The result was to create a kind of common law of Catholic morality, converting the so-called moral law into a kind of positive law, into a kind of new system of Mosaic law, this in spite of the fact that St. Paul had insisted so strongly that the moral order of the Christian, while firm and demanding, does not have the character of a religious legalism. And on this point the viewpoint of Paul derives directly from that of Jesus when he said: "The sabbath was made for man, not man for the sabbath." (Mk. 2:27).

Unlike a morality of "principles," which gives all the proper stress to the role of the personal conscience in the determination of the moral life of each person, the morality of "propositions" as practiced in the Catholic Church left this function excessively in the shade. This happened because Catholics, on the basis of an overstrict and excessively uncritical understanding of the normative value of the moral (not infallible) magisterium of the Church and of the role of the priest in the sacrament of penance, practically eliminated the function of the conscience. The priest was the conscience of the believer. The ordinary magisterium of the Holy See and the moral theology books were the conscience of the priest. In this way, conscience had disappeared.

That is one of the reasons for the present crisis of moral conscience among Christians, particularly the young, and particularly on issues of sexual morality. We had failed to educate the consciences of the faithful by open discussion with them. Instead, we had tried to make them absolutely responsive in passive obedience to whatever the priest might tell them. Now the young people have lost confidence in what the priest says and in what the noninfallible magisterium of the Holy See says, and because they have not been helped to form a truly personal conscience, they have become disoriented and are exposed to the danger of falling into an almost total state of amorality.

The remedy is to change the direction toward a solid moral training in "principles," stressing the primary and inescapable role of personal conscience.

What we call the natural moral law (although it is not properly and strictly "natural") cannot provide a closed system of norms of conduct capable of being formulated in statically defined "propositions" that could become a "code" of conduct valid always and everywhere, such as the text of a law once written for all time and afterward subject only to casuistic interpretation.

The structure of the moral law, as a guide to determining what is wrong and setting up rules of conduct, is quite different. It belongs to the order of "principles," and these moral principles are not purely "formal" ones. A purely formal principle would be, for example, the principle of justice, if the claim were then made that anything might be ruled just, because the notion of justice would thereby be reduced to a pure mental "form," entirely neutral as regards the possible material content. Under such a supposition, the concept of "justice" would be radically variable and entirely conditioned by the arbitrariness of the individual will or by the blind mechanism of social forces.

The principles of the moral law are not of that kind. We can rather conceive of them as "value guides" in the field of values that have a material content. They are neither purely "formal" nor of the static rigidity of a "proposition." They are much more open to the complexity of reality and of historic evolution; for example, respect for human dignity may make very different concrete demands in the thirteenth century and in the twentieth.

At the same time, nevertheless, the principles have the force (the normative pressure) of a value guide in an area of values with a demanding material content.

To the extent that they are "value guides," the principles have to be translated in some way into propositions, that is to say, into concrete norms of conduct that will express in practice, to be applied in lived situations, the values indicated in the principles.

Some "limit propositions" of a mostly negative character (things that must in all circumstances be avoided) and expressing certain concrete demands that are valid for every time and circumstance may perhaps be established in the light of the principles. But such "limit propositions" will surely be very few.

As a general rule, the propositions into which the moral demands indicated by the principles can and should be translated will be relative to the historic time and to the social and geographic situation. They are propositions conditioned simultaneously by the principles themselves (which are demanding "value guides") and by the circumstances given historically and socially. The "propositions" represent an effort of the human spirit (of the "moral conscience") to integrate and apply the moral principles to the concrete human reality, which is essentially historic and social, thus giving a living content in history and in human society to that "spark of wisdom" (*scintilla mentis*, in the poetic expression of theologians of the distant past) of which the moral law consists.

I might add that the possibility of knowing these moral propositions governing conduct is often not independent of certain "choices" of the human conscience, which is not simply the passive recorder of something that has been given to it as a whole. These choices, on the one hand, cannot be arbitrary, but must rather represent the "response" to a "call" that comes from reality, from the real "meaning" of existence. They should, in addition, be a projection of the inner light (of the moral wisdom of the "principles"). On the other hand, however, the content of the propositions cannot be established by a Cartesian method of starting from a kind of intellectual contemplation of the needs of an objective order of what might be called Platonic essences. Here an inductive element, a reflection on one's own experience in life, comes into play. But neither can a scientific analysis of structures or a sociological analysis give us a fully formed morality. An element of "risk" always remains, a risk that is correlative to the inescapable personal "responsibility" of the moral life.

Human dialogue, and also for Christians ecclesial dialogue, has a role to play in the construction of these "propositions." This is the point at which a pastoral service of the ordinary magisterium is properly introduced. But just as—apart from the case of possible (but very rare) "limit propositions"—the moral "propositions" have some historical, cultural, and sociological relativity, so also in turn they can prove not to be applicable to specific concrete cases. It can also happen that a person may have valid reasons in conscience for not accepting a "proposition" that is commonly admitted in the cultural (ecclesiastical or civil) environment to which he belongs. Here the final decision lies with his conscience, provided it is truly sincere (a right conscience). And the more personal (intimate) the moral problem is, the more personal must be the search and the decision on the concrete proposition determining conduct; for the principles, as "value guides" that can never be set aside, are the only absolute element.

The "principles," however, unlike the "propositions," are essentially "open." They cannot be satisfactorily reduced to a static and clearly fixed proposition. It follows from this that the value guides of distinct principles may come together to decide a concrete problem. And a dialectic tension may at times arise between them, when it would seem that to follow the line of some of them would place us in contradiction to the orientation of others. In this way, the morality of "principles" restores its value to the inescapable role of the personal conscience, because the synthesis of the various values in a concrete situation, particularly in a complex one, can never be done once and for all. It has to be repeated each time in the light of a right conscience, which sincerely seeks not to betray any of the basic values, while seeking at the same time to remain open to a reality that can be very complex both on the personal level and on the social level.

It seems to me that the reference the Second Vatican Council makes to the natural law in the Pastoral Constitution on the Church in the Modern World (Gaudium et spes), No. 16, which significantly is included in the teaching on conscience, is basically pointed toward a morality of "principles" in the sense in which I present it:

In the depths of his conscience, man detects a law which he does not impose upon himself, but which holds him to obedience. Always summoning him to love good and avoid evil, the voice of conscience can when necessary speak to his heart more specifically: Do this, shun that. For man has in his heart a law written by God. To obey it is the very dignity of man; according to it he will be judged. Conscience is the most secret core and sanctuary of a man. There he is alone with God, whose voice echoes in his depths. In a wonderful manner conscience reveals that law which is fulfilled by love of God and neighbor. In fidelity to conscience, Christians are joined with the rest of men in the search for truth, and for the generous solution to the numerous problems which arise in the life of individuals and from social relationships. Hence the more that a correct conscience holds sway, the more persons and groups turn aside from blind choice and strive to be guided by objective norms of morality. Conscience frequently errs from invincible ignorance without losing its dignity. The same cannot be said of a man who cares but little for truth and goodness, or of a conscience which by degrees grows practically sightless as a result of habitual sin.

The primacy of the personal conscience and of the personal discovery of the moral norm over the dictates of a socially established morality does not mean that the study of works of moral theology is worthless. But it should be brought back to its true meaning. What is involved is to continue in this responsible search for the true and the good, to throw light with due discernment on the "call" that God makes in the depth of man's conscience.

In an analogous sense, the authentic magisterium of the Catholic ecclesiastical hierarchy concerning the demands of the moral law known as natural, which is to say not "revealed," should not be understood as the "promulgation" of a divine law, but as an authorized though not infallible teaching concerning the meaning of this call of conscience. This magisterium is not a substitute for conscience; it is (or should be) an aid in reading that voice of conscience. The search for truth and good, which man may never cease, if his conscience is to retain the dignity of the "call" of God, must grant—among Catholics—its due worth to this non-infallible magisterium of the Church, neither more nor less. But in the final analysis, the means of "promulgation" (to use the word in a very analogical sense) of the natural moral law is the personal conscience and it alone. The reason is that the natural moral law, as the Constitution on the Church in the Modern World says, following St. Paul, is a law written by God in the heart of man. The suggestive expression of Paul is that those who are not subject to the law of Moses show, in the testimony of their conscience, the *effective* equivalent of the law, the substance of the law (*tò érgon toû nómou*: Rm. 2:15). It is a fact, however, that only God writes on man's heart.

If then we agree that the natural moral law belongs radically to the order of "principles," not of "propositions," the same must be said with far more reason, if that is possible, when we talk about what we can call the "evangelical law." To attempt to reduce the "evangelical law" to an order of what might be called frozen "principles," to be applied casuistically, is to turn into a dead-end street. The moral order of the Christian is strong and demanding. It is completely removed from any kind of ethical legalism. St. Paul stressed this point with all his power, especially in his Letters to the Galatians and to the Romans.

It is undeniable that evangelical morality is a morality of "principles." St. Paul states that love of the neighbor is the entirety of the law (Rm. 13:8–10). But the law of love is essentially a dynamic principle. Love cannot be reduced to "propositions." In this context, the following passage from St. Augustine is highly stimulating:

> The diverse intention therefore makes the things done diverse. Though the thing be one, yet if we measure it by the diverse intentions, we find the one a thing to be loved, the other to be condemned; the one we find a thing to be glorified, the other to be detested. Such is the force of charity. See that it alone discriminates, it alone distinguishes the doings of men.
>
> This we have said in the case where the things done are similar. In the case where they are diverse, we find a man by charity made fierce; and by iniquity made winningly gentle. A father beats a boy, and a boy-stealer caresses. If thou name the two things, blows and caresses, who would not choose the caresses and decline the blows? If thou mark the persons, it is charity that beats, iniquity that caresses. See what we are insisting upon; that the deeds of men are only discerned by the root of charity. For many things may be done that have a good appearance, and yet proceed not from the root of charity. For thorns also have flowers; some actions truly seem rough, seem savage; howbeit they are done for discipline at the bidding of charity. Once for all, then, a short precept is given thee: Love, and do what thou wilt; whether thou hold thy peace, through love hold thy peace; whether thou cry out, through love cry out; whether thou correct, through love correct; whether thou spare, through love do thou spare: Let the root of love be within, of this root can nothing spring but what is good.[1]

[1] In epist. Ioannis, 7, 7–8; P.L. 35, 2033. English translation from Nicene and Post-Nicene Fathers, Philip Schaff, ed., Vol. VII (Grand Rapids, Mich.: William B. Eerdmans, 1956), p. 504.

These remarkable words of St. Augustine give us the fundamental answer to the question: What are the moral principles that can guide a man in the development of his sexual life? (It is paradoxical in the extreme that this help should come from—of all people—St. Augustine, who in his notions of sex never succeeded in freeing himself existentially from Manichaeanism and exercised a very negative influence on Christian moral theology. This once again demonstrates the enormous complexity of the Christian phenomenon in history.)

The ruling principle of all sexual morality cannot be other than the love of our neighbor as ourselves. And as St. Paul says, referring not only to the sex life but to the whole of human morality, all we need is that principle.

All the other principles must always be an extension, a consequence, an "explanation," or a condition of this one.

We can safely say—and this may get rid of some misunderstandings—that man cannot leave his sexuality abandoned to the blind play of instinctive impulses. Man's instinct, because of his creative imagination and his power of projection, does not have the self-balancing quality that may be found in that of other animals. We have to admit the principle that some controls, a margin of restraint and of sublimation of the sexual instinct, are needed for the right ordering of the person, both in himself and in his availability to open up to others in authentic interpersonal love: to love the neighbor as himself.

The principle of love, as ruler of human sexual morality, seems to me capable of being developed into the following principles:

1. The sexual activity between two participants should always be exercised as a "mediation" of an interpersonal, respectful love, worthy to be called such. One's partner should not be reduced to the level of an "object" of exploitation and of selfish enjoyment, even in a situation in which the enjoyment would be selfish on both sides and agreed to by both parties. That would not be the same thing as interpersonal love. And a sex encounter without love is something inhuman, and in the end, sad and disappointing.

When Jesus says to us, "If a man looks at a woman lustfully, he has already committed adultery with her in his heart" (Mt. 5:28), the deeper meaning of his words is directed to forbidding this lowering of the other person to the level of an "object" of exploitation and enjoyment, even if the process stays in the man's heart; because true love of the neighbor is then negated in the heart.

If sexuality is to be exercised as a "mediation" of an interpersonal love, it must be said that full sexual activity demands a very high and full level of interpersonal love: the participation and unreserved surrender to each other of two persons; a very deep love. In this sense it can be said that a common bed requires a common table. The *connubium* involves the *convivium:* a total living together. It seems indeed that the physical and emotional weight of the complete sexual relationship is so great that, if it is not integrated into a community of interpersonal love at a sufficiently deep level, it will very easily fall into the selfishness of exploitation of an "object" of pleasure. That is the inner meaning of the biblical statement that the man and woman "become one body" (Gn. 2:24). The most intense carnal unity becomes integrated into a total unity.

2. The interpersonal vital unity that integrates full sexual unity and makes it truly human and good carries with it a title to "faithfulness."

3. If sexuality, at whatever level it expresses itself, is to be integrated into a genuine interpersonal love and be purified of the tendency to reduce the partner to the level of an "object" of pleasure, this sexuality must be lived at all levels within a framework of respect for the dignity of the other person. This is merely the principle of love viewed from a different angle.

These three principles can be concretely seen reflected in a series of very beautiful biblical texts. Scripture condemns prostitution and adultery in the strongest terms, while describing married love

in words of charming freshness and free of any strain of the gray
and forbidding puritanism with which a whole current of tradition has tended to portray "conjugal chastity."

I would like to insert here the texts that seem to me most inspired:

> Drink the water from your own cistern,
>   fresh water from your own well.
> Do not let your fountains flow to waste elsewhere,
>   nor your streams in the public streets.
> Let them be for yourself alone,
>   not for strangers at the same time.
> And may your fountainhead be blessed!
> Find joy with the wife you married in your youth,
>   fair as a hind, graceful as a fawn.
> Let hers be the company you keep,
> hers the breasts that ever fill you with delight,
>   hers the love that ever holds you captive.
>
> (Pr. 5:15–19)

> Do not turn against a wise and good wife,
>   for her charm is worth more than gold.
>
> (Si. 7:19)

> Like the sun rising over the mountains of the Lord
>   is the beauty of a good wife in a well-kept house.
> Like the lamp shining on the sacred lampstand
>   is a beautiful face on a well-proportioned body.
> Like golden pillars on a silver base
>   are shapely legs on firm-set heels.
>
> (Si. 26:16–18)

> A woman's beauty delights the beholder,
>   a man likes nothing better.
> If her tongue be kind and gentle,
>   her husband has no equal among the sons of men.

173

The man who takes a wife has the makings of a fortune,
a helper that suits him, and a pillar to lean on.
If a property has no fence, it will be plundered.
When a man has no wife, he is aimless and querulous.
Will anyone trust a man carrying weapons
who flits from town to town?
So it is with the man who has no nest,
and lodges wherever night overtakes him.

(Si. 36:22–27)

Even St. Paul, who—as we saw above—seems to have had a somewhat biased and negative understanding of marriage, speaks warmly of the warmth of love of husband and wife: "Husbands must love their wives as they love their own bodies; for a man to love his wife is for him to love himself. A man never hates his own body, but he feeds it and looks after it. . . . For this reason, a man must leave his father and mother and be joined to his wife, and the two will become one body." (Ep. 5:28–29 and 31).

In the first Letter to the Thessalonians, the condemnation of fornication is linked to the positive idea of respect for the body (of the human, embodied person), probably of the partner: "What God wants is for you all to be holy. He wants you to keep away from fornication, and each one of you to know how to use the body that belongs to him [the "body" here referred to is probably that of his wife] in a way that is holy and honorable, not giving way to selfish lust like the pagans who do not know God. He wants nobody at all ever to sin by taking advantage of a brother in these matters; the Lord always punishes sins of that sort, as we told you before and assured you. We have been called by God to be holy, not to be immoral; in other words, anyone who objects is not objecting to a human authority, but to God, who gives you his Holy Spirit." (I Th. 4:3–8). Similarly the first Letter of St. Peter (3:7) urges husbands to treat their wives with consideration and respect.

In his book, *But That I Can't Believe* (New York: New

American Library, 1967), Anglican Bishop John A. Robinson has some thoughts full of wisdom about the application of the principle of love to sexual morality in the contemporary social context. I want to include them here because I am in total agreement.

I want people to be *free*—to decide responsibly for themselves what *love* at its deepest really requires of them. But there could hardy be anything further from that than free love—which is usually neither love nor free.

Consider, for instance, this conversation from the film *Room at the Top*:

"I do love you," she protests; "I would do anything for you." "Sure," he retorts, "you would do anything—except the one thing that any girl would do for the man she loves." So she succumbs—the victim of emotional blackmail.

That's not love. It's much more fear than love—fear of losing him if she doesn't.

Under that sort of fear people are not free. And thousands of young people today are simply being played upon in this matter of sex.

Their emotions are exploited by the advertisers. Glamour is commercialized. They can't afford not to go along with the rest. "Dread of being a social outcast is the main reason why teenagers have sexual intercourse before marriage," writes a girl student in *Sixth Form Opinion*.

I want a morality which frees people from that. But I know we shan't get it by simply saying "Thou shalt not!" a bit louder.

Young people today ask "Why?"—and quite rightly. They want a basis for morality that makes sense in terms of personal relationships. They want *honesty* in sex, as in everything else.

And that's what chastity is. It isn't just abstinence. It's honesty in sex: having physical relationships that *truthfully* express what's there underneath.

Sex—and this applies inside marriage just as much as out of it—which doesn't really express love is an immoral sham.

But what is love? It's giving yourself to the other person, completely and without condition, for his or her own sake. It's wanting to share your whole life, without keeping anything back.

Sex is the most intimate and wonderful expression of this deep sharing of life with life. To use it for kicks—or out of fear of being thought a square—when there's nothing there behind it is a fearful desecration.

But suppose there *is* something there? Suppose you are deeply in love, but can't get married?

I would say: "Be absolutely honest with yourself." Even if you're engaged, you can't really share everything. Bed without board *is* a cheat—especially for the girl. If you *really* love her, you'll think twice—and twice again. For it's bound to be less than the best.

But it's your decision. I'm not going to take it for you or take it from you. I can know what love demands of me. But, no more than Jesus, am I going to throw the first stone into other people's lives—though I can do my utmost to save them from messing them up.

I believe that young people today are genuinely looking for a morality that cuts deeper, is more searching and less superficial than the ready-made rules of their parents—honored in any case more in the breach than in the observance. . . .

And in all this they desperately need *help*, not condemnation. I prefer to keep my condemnation for:

1. Those who exploit sex for gain—especially under the nauseating hypocrisy of "exposing vice."
2. Those who tell the young that they can't be "with it" unless they "have sex."
3. Those who treat sex simply as a game (which is different from saying that there is a playful element in it to be enjoyed).
4. Those who snigger at it as dirty or moralize about it as sin.
5. Those who report what responsible people say as though they were advocating immorality or condoning laxity.
6. Those who weigh in with a heavy hand on the basis of such press reports.

Finally, I want to *commend* those who are trying to hammer out real standards for their lives amid so many more pressures than we were exposed to. And I want to commend those—only too few—who are prepared to give of their time to get alongside them in schools and clubs, at home and in church, in clinics and counseling.

For this is where any new morality must be thrashed out which is really going to be worth anything.

I want to add two further points about the principles of sexual morality:

1. The principle of integration of full sexual activity into a communion of the partners' interpersonal love and life is closely intertwined with the principle of genetic fruitfulness. The fullness of a mutual personal, erotic, and sexual love tends to express itself in the fruit of this love, in the child of the couple. The child is like an integration of the parents being "two in one body." But this fruitfulness, because it is human, must be responsible, and in consequence limited. Its perfection is measured qualitatively rather than quantitatively. It is not necessary to have many children, but to have true fruits and signs of love.

2. Sexual self-control at the level of each individual's dealings with himself (control of imaginative eroticism or of the possibilities of sexual orgasm, for example) should be determined not according to strict propositions based on what might be called a "physiologistic" concept, but according to a principle that is less concerned with the purely material and specifically human elements than with the basic principle of love. The issue is not to condemn absolutely as fiendish every sensation of sexual pleasure and every ejaculation that are not involuntary, but to maintain firmly this orientation: At the level of each individual's own dealings with sex, he should avoid whatever might lessen his availability for love of others or what might upset the equilibrium of his personality, which would also affect his availability for love of others. I believe sincerely, and I express my belief with a conscience fully at peace, that all that is necessary is to be faithful to this principle. With such fidelity (if sincere), one can be sure of avoiding self-centered licentiousness, without the danger of falling into intolerable tensions that would be enslaving rather than liberating, and that I do not believe to be in accord with God's will.

Before ending this chapter, I want to come back a moment for further reflection on the "charism" of celibacy for the sake of the Kingdom of God.

What is the "meaning" of this charism?

It is often said that it is to make the man more available for service to others. That reason does not convince me. If I compare doctors and priests, for example, I do not find the celibate priest more available for his service than the married doctor is for his.

I find some elements of guidance, however, when I look more deeply into St. Paul's teaching in the first Letter to the Corinthians on marriage and virginity, in spite of the limitations that seem to affect the Pauline text.

St. Paul says: "An unmarried man can devote himself to the Lord's affairs, all he need worry about is pleasing the Lord; but a married man has to bother about the world's affairs and devote himself to pleasing his wife: He is torn two ways." (I Co. 7:32–34).

St. Paul's view is one-sided and is not very convincing for many of us. By devoting himself to pleasing his wife, at the level of a truly Christian love, the married man can please God just as much as the celibate does. And if the celibate becomes too unconcerned about the world's affairs, that is to say, too unconcerned about a realistic and incarnated love of others, his concern about pleasing God may well become an illusion. The parable of the Good Samaritan (Lk. 10:25–37) gives some hints along these lines. And St. John's first Letter states the message clearly: "A man that does not love the brother that he can see cannot love God, whom he has never seen." (I Jn. 4:20).

This does not mean, nevertheless, that we cannot get some guidance if we search for the deeper meaning of St. Paul's statement.

What is valid in this statement is that the celibate for the sake of the Kingdom of God relates to God in a different way than those who are married.

A married man must come to God "in" his love for his wife. If that love is perfect, then it constitutes an open dynamism of love. In the experience of married love, which when perfect is not a lesser "charism" than that of genuine (perfect) celibacy for the sake of the Kingdom of God, the Christian spouse lives his love of God and makes himself available for an unlimited love of others, just like the Samaritan in the parable. Married love, when truly deep, Christian, and "charismatic," is a school of love that makes the spouses available to love and to pardon (to love that extends even to enemies).

The celibate for the sake of the Kingdom of God also has to reach God "in" love of others; because if he does not, he will not reach him. The text of St. John's Letter eliminates all doubt on that issue. But to reach God he does not have the experience of married love, and this leaves an emptiness in him. Before the account of Eve's creation in Genesis, God is made to say: "It is not good that the man should be alone. I will make him a helpmate." (Gn. 2:18). And as we have seen, Ben Sirach—author of the book known as Ecclesiasticus—held a negative view of "the man who has no nest, and lodges wherever night overtakes him" (Si. 36:27). He is talking about the celibate.

Looked at in this perspective, the "charism" of the celibate for the sake of the Kingdom of God is a gift that makes it possible for the celibate (man or woman) to live the lack of married love without falling into the alienation characteristic of the "bachelor," which is in the order of selfishness, bitterness, resentment, and inability to love humanly and joyously. And what saves the charismatic celibate from falling into such alienation is what God means in his life.

The "loneliness" of the celibate tends to sterility: "It is not good that the man should be alone." The experience of the charismatic celibate for the sake of the Kingdom of God is that he *is not alone.*

Within the extreme modesty of my spiritual experiences, I dare to say that I am witness to that fact.

The married man, whose marriage is successful, when he closes the door of his room at the end of his day's toil, is not alone. He breathes and grows in the precious intimacy he shares with his wife. It is good for him not to be alone.

In a similar way, though I am no mystic, I do not live the pain of being alone when I shut my room door. I live a "not being alone." This is my celibacy for the sake of the Kingdom of God.

The charism of this celibacy is, so to say, not given for a specific reason. It is not utilitarian. Its purpose is not to enable us to work more. This charism merely serves to signify. It is an eschatological sign.

I am not more perfect than a married man. I do not love God more or better than the married man who loves him "in" his love for his wife. The only difference is that I love God with a distinct modality. The spouse (who is Christian and charismatic) encounters God "in" his spouse, whereas I encounter him in the vacuum of not having a spouse. And this encounter frees me from the alienating loneliness of the "bachelor." And as for the husband, the love of his wife (and for the wife, the love of her husband) is the school in which he learns to love his neighbor, similarly for me this tenuous experience of not being alone in my being without a spouse, this way of relating to God, is the school of learning to love others.

The "charism" of celibacy for the sake of the Kingdom of God is not better than the "charism" of married love. It is different. And it is interesting. It has something of mystery in it. For that reason, it is a sign. Charismatic married love is also a "sign." They are distinct signs. In this diversity is seen the immensity of the Spirit.

To live the life of celibacy for the sake of the Kingdom of God is a beautiful experience when one has the "charism" that makes it possible. It is a "gift." I am happy with it. I do not envy married people. And I do not think that they should envy me. For if they do not realize fully the ideal of Christian and human marriage, neither do I succeed in realizing fully the ideal of celibacy for the sake of the Kingdom of God. The ideal is never realized exhaustively in this life. But when we at least go forward on our way in its light, our lives are full of meaning.

V

Life and Death

In October 1971, as I approached my sixtieth birthday (having been born at Gijón, Spain, on October 22, 1911), symptoms of paralysis developed in my right leg, and also some slight problems in my right arm. After a long and penetrating clinical study of the symptoms, Professor Alemá, head of the neurology department of the Hospital of St. Camillus in Rome, made a definite diagnosis of inflammation of the marrow of the spine resulting from cervical spondylosis, a condition capable of correction by surgery. In less technical language, I had a fusion of four vertebrae of the cervix, and the squeezing of the bony substance on the marrow caused the pain. On December 16, Dr. Bravo, head of the section of neurosurgery of the Puerta de Hierro Clinic in Madrid, operated on me most skillfully, working on the joints of vertebrae Nos. 5 and 6. Twelve days later, he performed an extensive cutting of the cervical layers of vertebrae Nos. 4 and 7, thereby easing the pressure. The result was to free me from the paralysis and restore my ability to do my regular work. I take this opportunity to thank both doctors.

About a month passed between the time when the symptoms indicated that a serious disturbance of the marrow existed and the doctor's decision that a cure existed for the disease. During that interval, I was faced by two possibilities, both of them probable. One, which subsequently proved to have been correct, was that a remedy for the condition would be found. The other, equally probable until the diagnosis was completed, was that I was suffering from an internal degenerative process of the marrow for which medical science had not so far found a cure. That would mean a total paralysis of arms and legs leading to an early death.

I was quite clear about all of this. And the uncertainty continued for approximately a month.

I was consequently compelled to face the problem of death (of my death) with a realism and an immediacy I had never before had occasion to experience.

The real, concrete, and immediate possibility of death produced, as its first impact, a slight shiver of fear.

Catholic children have had drilled into their consciousness and subconsciousness from infancy such a fear of judgment and hell that it is hard not to have some development of this anxiety when faced with a real and concrete prospect of death.

I succeeded, nevertheless, in getting over this first reaction easily, I might even say in a single stroke. I pray God that this freedom will stay solidly with me when death does in fact come.

I freed myself from this shiver of fear simply because for many years the conviction that fear of hell is un-Christian was rooted deeply in me.

I do not dismiss the teaching on hell or the fear of hell, provided these concepts are seriously purified from the residue of surrealist specters carved around the tops of medieval Romanesque columns.

But I have the impression that the complex of "fear" of hell has been far more an instrument of "power" of the clergy than a means for advancing the religious and moral life of the faithful. This does not mean that the clergy did not often use this instrument in good faith, and that they were not themselves equally caught in the web of those terrors.

The ideas that the God of the oppressed will work justice and that what he can do goes beyond the visible plane of history are very serious ones. The man of faith lives these beliefs. They are the beliefs that those who have created the structures of wrong-doing will one day have to face the triumph of justice, witnessing their own defeat:

> Clearly we have strayed from the way of truth
> the light of justice has not shone for us,
> the sun never rose on us.
> We have left no path of lawlessness or ruin unexplored,
> we have crossed deserts where there was no track,
> but the way of the Lord is one we have never known.
>
> (Ws. 5:6–7)

It is the idea that Jesus is the Lord, that the "powers" will be overcome, and that the Lord will have the last word.

But the way in which all this will occur is completely hidden from us.

Our attitude should not be one of fear of hell, but rather of deep humility, like that of the tax collector in St. Luke's Gospel (18:9–14), and of hope and hunger for justice. Those alone are appropriate for anyone who has believed with any degree of sincerity in Jesus.

Once I had overcome this tremor of fear of hell, I was able to face calmly the situation created for me by the very concrete possibility of a quick death.

The first step in this existential reflection was not to suppress what I might call the reality of death by the simple substitution of the idea of the "other" life.

Perhaps influenced by the spiritual situation of the Christians of our time who properly resist an infantile and trite use of the "hereafter" as a device to close one's eyes to the seriousness and weight of the "here and now," I felt myself spontaneously drawn to face death from "this side."

I did not for a moment deny the transcendence (the mystery of hope), which is for me necessary to life, even to the marrow

183

of my bones and for all time. But I did not simply transfer myself to "the other side." Instead, I remained face to face with death. Of course, I was not without transcendental hope. But I believe that my refusal to insist on that aspect was also sincere, my stand with my feet fixed firmly on this earth, facing up to death in this way. The fact is that transcendental hope is "a dark light" (a mystery), whereas death was standing in front of me as a tangible reality. I tried not to close my eyes, to face death positively.

I offer here the results of this existential experience. To what extent this experience is valid to its innermost depths (an existential reality, not a conceptual construction) I will not know until I repeat the experience in the precise moment when death actually takes place for me. The experience has, in any case, been valuable for me. And certainly, in the circumstances in which I found myself, I am sure the responses were far more than empty talk; for, as a matter of fact, the probability of death was facing me in a concrete and immediate way, and I felt at peace. There was consequently an element of existential truth in my experience.

I was not sad at dying. I don't mean that I wanted to die, either from a boredom with life, which I did not and do not feel, or from the kind of mystic elation that made St. Paul say, "I want to be gone and be with Christ." (Ph. 1:23). I was facing death without mysticism.

It did not grieve me to die. More than that, I was up to a point happy to die then, although I would also be happy not to die, and now I am happy that I did not die.

Why did the prospect of death not make me sad?

The reason was fundamentally this. During my entire life, ever since I entered the novitiate on August 15, 1930, and placed myself in closer contact than previously with the Gospel, I had succeeded in recognizing—in a semiformulated way and in spite of a thousand obstacles—that to be with Jesus was to be effectively with the poor and the oppressed. But my status within the ecclesiastical "apparatus," and specifically within the apparatus of "the states of perfection" as a member of a religious community, provided me with no opportunity to exercise such an option in a concrete way. This had been a frustration of which I was always to some extent aware.

Athough only to a very small extent, and more at the verbal level than anything else, I had in the past sixteen years been able to move some distance in the desired direction. Through my work as a teacher and lecturer, I had made a small contribution to the efforts to start a cultural revolution in the Church in order that the Christianity lived by Christians would become ethicoprophetic, and their attitude toward the revolutionary process of liberating the oppressed would come one day to correspond with a genuine faith in Jesus Christ.

All this work has been a mere trifle, shot through with all the ambiguities of the "compromised intellectual." But I do believe it was something real. In addition, it has not been academic. From the age of forty-four to fifty-nine, I have lived with working people, slept in shacks, shared camp bed dormitories with young workers. We saw each other as brothers. I have learned from the workers just as I have learned from young college students, from unbelievers open to the love of men, and from "progressive Christians."

These past sixteen years of my life have made a qualitative change in my biography.

Since, in addition, I am convinced of my own slight worth (of what "great things" I am incapable of doing), the ability to have succeeded in what little I have done I regard as a "gift," a precious "grace." I see this the more clearly because my success in doing these things resulted from no heroic action on my part, no superman ability in overcoming the cultural and structural obstacles blocking the way, but rather from a fortunate combination of circumstances and—I believe—the action of the Spirit of Christ in my heart. In a word, there was something that was "given" to me. And this something has been for me of great worth.

I accordingly thought to myself: Taking into account how little I am, what more can I expect from life than to have been able to do this, which—taking my circumstances into account—has been almost a miracle, a small miracle like myself?

I thought of a very ordinary example, one that nevertheless held for me the power to express a great deal, and that helped to fix my feelings in the attitude of deep peace with which I lived my experience of the prospect of imminent death. I said to myself: If somebody gives you a beautiful box of candies, would it not be absurd to start crying because it is a one-pound and not a two-pound box? Once you recognize that there has to be some limit to the size of the box, if the candies are good, the only reasonable response when the box is empty is pleasure for having enjoyed them. Thus I, having lived a life that had "meaning," have only the joy of having lived it.

Death for me, seen from "this side"—that is to say, without stressing transcendent hope—presented itself in a very positive way as fitting into the category of "rest," of "sleep," of the "Sabbath pause." Modern activism, turning even one's vacation into a time of mad activity, has lost to a great extent this concept of "rest," which is so deeply biblical, and which Genesis, Exodus, and Deuteronomy apply even to God: "He rested from the work he had performed."

It is true that the divine rest is not conceived as sleep, but as the quiet contemplation and enjoyment of the work done. But it is also enjoyable to enter into the rest of sleep, leaving behind the finished task.

An element in this experience of facing death peacefully has proved important for me. The peaceful and fully human and positive acceptance of death does not need to rest on an afterlife. It can (and should) be sustained on what is left behind, fundamentally on the life led in love of others, in what there can have sincerely been of "hunger and thirst for justice."

There is something here that leaves me perplexed. What made it possible for me to face death peacefully, without histrionics, without losing the inner joy of my life, was fundamentally that I had lived—I believe with some sincerity—in the love of others. The joy of the life I had lived, which did not grow less with the prospect of death, was rooted in the existential (imperfect, yet real) experience of the love of the brotherhood. That being so, how could I look with such peace on a death that meant separation from those loved ones?

In actual fact so many of my friends had felt such anguish at the prospect of my possible death that I wanted not to die when I took this aspect into account, because what was not unpleasant for me (but rather a tempting prospect of "rest") was for them a cause for sadness, and for some of really profound sadness.

But why did this separation not represent for me a break with tragic overtones?

I believe that at this point I did indeed have present and dominant my faith in the resurrection—in Jesus Christ—and my eschatological hope, which crosses over like an anchor to the other side of death and reaches (with closed eyes) the "afterlife." But it is a hope that is not centered on apocalyptic illusions (even if those in the Apocalypse of St. John are so beautiful and of such profound symbolism), but rather in the experience of Christian love, which is authentic human love open to the infinite: the revelation of Jesus on earth.

St. Paul has written: "Love does not come to an end." (I Co. 13:8). And St. John says: "We have passed out of death and into life, and of this we can be sure because we love our brothers." (I Jn. 3:14).

My firm eschatological hope is centered not on a "myth," but on an "experience": the experience of having begun to learn humbly what it means to love others and to hunger after justice.

For that reason, faced with the concrete possibility of imminent death, I felt joyous.

And I end this book proclaiming that I BELIEVE IN HOPE.

Rome
July 15 to September 30, 1972